GIBGATE

The Untold Story

by

WILLIAM
FLYNN

Dublin
September 1992

First published in 1992 by
Celtic Publishing Ltd.,
27 Athol Street, Douglas,
Isle of Man

ISBN 0 9520309 0 X

Photographs courtesy The Phoenix, Sunday Business Post, Fianna Fail & Fine Gael Press Offices, The Guardian and The Sunday Tribune.

Printed in Great Britain.

Special Acknowledgement to Sean Boyne, Dave Mullins and Cathal O'Shea of the Sunday World for their coverage of I.L.L. collapse in June 1984.

To my wife Eileen

And

all who stood by me.

Contents

"When money speaks, the truth keeps silents"
-Russian proverb

Introduction

My name is Billy Flynn. I am a private investigator.

Paint a picture in your mind of a typical member of my profession. He probably wears a slouch hat and a raincoat with its collar pulled up. He chain-smokes, carries a gun and is never stuck for a cynical wisecrack. Trouble is his business.

Now banish that picture to the world of the films where it belongs. We're not like that. I'm not like that - apart from the chain-smoking.

So what am I like? I am 47 years old. I am married with five daughters and three sons, and was in the motor trade before starting in my current business. I live in County Meath, an hour's drive from Dublin. I have been a lifelong supporter of Fianna Fail. The only details you need to know about my personality for the purposes of this story are that I am stubborn by nature and have a natural distrust of the establishment.

I also loathe injustice. Especially when its victims are in no position to fight back.

Don't get me wrong - I am no crusader. I entered this profession purely and simply to make money. But the case that for the last eight years has taken over my life hasn't earned me a penny. On the contrary - I estimate it has cost me £500,000. It has also made me one of the most hated individuals among Ireland's legal and business fraternity. You think I'm exaggerating? Try mentioning the name Billy Flynn to the next Dublin barrister you meet.

The story you are about to read involves an audacious swindle by a charming con-man which caused financial ruin for hundreds of elderly people. Such cases, unfortunately, are nothing new - you read about them in the papers all the time. But what makes this fraud unique in Irish fiscal history is the time and effort spent trying to cover it up.

The case I have named **Gibgate** involves dirty tricks at the highest levels of Irish Government. It involves perversion of the course of justice, fraud and forgery within the "old boys' network" that makes up Dublin's legal and business community. It also involves me - although, at first, I didn't want to get involved.

What was to become an obsession began on May 26, 1984, when the phone rang in my office. On the line was a stranger, Frank Kelly from Birmingham. He had invested his life savings of £7,000 in a Dublin-based, Gibraltar-registered company called International Investments, and his money now seemed to have disappeared. Could I find out what had happened to it?

Up to then, I had been involved only in professional negligence work, and had no knowledge of offshore banking. I apologised to Kelly, saying it wasn't really my field.

Kelly called back again and again, insisting he needed my help, until I lost my temper and told him in no uncertain terms to leave me alone. But, finally, I relented - the man sounded desperate - and I agreed to make some enquiries.

If I'd known what I was taking on, I would have stuck to negligence cases. In the eight years since that phone call, my fight for justice for the victims of a crooked financier named Finbarr Ross has taken me all over the world. It has driven me to drink and a heart attack, caused me to neglect my family and bankrupted me twice.

At the start of the case I had visions of an astronomical commission, but when it became obvious there was going to be little or no cash in it for me, I carried on regardless. I became a financial junkie, borrowing here and there to keep the thing on fire.

Why? If I hadn't become involved, the circumstances surrounding the collapse of International Investments Ltd. would have died a convenient death years ago - convenient, that is, for the many pillars of Dublin society who have a personal interest in seeing the facts buried. In the course of my investigation, I encountered so much corruption, deceit and plain greed at the highest levels that I knew I couldn't let this case go.

The fact that **Gibgate** hasn't yet become a national scandal is in itself a national scandal. This book will hopefully go some way towards rectifying that state of affairs. I hope you find it as gripping as you would any good detective tale - but I would ask you not to forget one important difference.

In this one, every word is true.

Chapter One

CHASING THE RAINBOW

Let me tell you about a crook named Finbarr Ross. I have never met the man, but in twelve years as a private investigator have come across many like him. I know the type all too well - charming, believable, totally without morals and incapable of feeling guilt. And above all, greedy.

Most of us are not like Finbarr Ross. Most of us wouldn't be able to sleep soundly in our beds if we knew we had brought financial ruin to hundreds of people. People who were guilty of nothing more than a desire to make their futures a little more secure.

But I don't imagine Ross hasn't lost a single night's sleep since the day in late 1983 when he absconded to Texas, leaving behind a sham finance company on the verge of collapse and its 1,200 helpless investors. Many were senior citizens who had entrusted their life savings to the corrupt Corkman, only to lose everything.

A total of £7 million went missing in the International Investments fraud. Not a penny of it has been recovered. In the words of one investor: "This man Ross is in America, and he is living off my money."

And what kind of life is he living? On October 20, 1991, beneath the headline **£7M FRAUD QUERY FINBARR FOUND IN U.S.**, the following story appeared on the front page of the Sunday Independent:

Finbarr Ross - the Cork-born financier wanted by police on fraud charges - is back in business and living the high life in Dallas (wrote reporter Mark Smith). **Acting on information I received from a Texas contact, I tracked Ross down to the Tipperary Inn, a favourite haunt of the city's Irish expatriates ...**

Forty-five year-old Ross lives in a luxury apartment in affluent North Dallas. He dresses in designer clothes and drives two cars. At the Tipperary Inn, he boasts of his polo-playing days in Dublin and buys drinks for anyone who'll listen to him. "He's obviously got a lot of money floating around", said a customer ...

Finbarr Ross has been in Dallas for two years. His business card carries the legend "G Finbarr Ross - Investment Banker". "I help people out of

bankruptcies", he says without a trace of irony. "I lend money to help start up companies. The only problem in my business is getting paid!"

"Come off it, Finbarr," joshes a friend, "you're a fucking millionaire!" Ross smiles contentedly but makes no comment; just takes another pull of his favourite Austrian vodka. "Dallas", he says, "is a great city" ...

When he pulls up outside the "Tip" in his black Corvette, registration CWX 476, and walks into the bar at 9 every evening, Finbarr takes centre-stage. He will make the rounds of the Budweiser drinkers perched on their bar-stools, slapping backs, cracking jokes, and more often than not, picking up the tab.

If he spots an attractive woman he will instruct the barman, Mullingar-born Gary, to give her a drink and tell her it's from Finbarr. And - who knows? The thrice-married Corkman may have made another conquest; he could charm a nun out of her habit ...

I ask Ross if he's ever done anything in business he's regretted. "Of course", he says. "When you make decisions on gut instinct like I do, you will make some mistakes. But if I've learnt one thing in life, it's that you should always think with the heart, not with the head. Go on what your heart tells you."

When I read that last line I was genuinely shocked by the man's audacity. Finbarr Ross thinking with the heart! It's not an organ he possesses.

I will freely admit I'm no angel. In my profession you can't afford to be. Like Ross, I have sometimes had to live beyond the law. Like Ross, I have made mistakes. And like Ross, I am fond of money. It's a rare man who isn't.

But, unlike Ross, I have never lined my pockets by callously cheating others. I have never conned my way into a lifestyle I don't deserve.

All parasites are motivated by greed, and Finbarr Ross, the baby-faced charmer from small-town Cork, is no exception. Greed has been his driving-force. Right from the beginning.

• • •

When George Finbarr Ross made his entrance into the world on September 21, 1945, his mother Eileen took one look at the screaming infant and thought "I am going to be proud of this boy". She already had a daughter, Anna, and was to have five further children, but from the moment of his birth Finbarr was her favourite. All through his childhood the doting Eileen ensured her oldest son had everything he wanted.

It wasn't easy. The Ross home was a small farm in Dunmanway, Co. Cork, and as the family grew larger their modest income began to feel the strain. Finbarr's father Nathaniel worked hard on his few acres of land, and Eileen ensured the children never went hungry. But it was a hand-to-mouth existence. Money would always be tight.

Despite Eileen's best efforts to ensure young Finbarr wanted for nothing, the boy was hard to please. He was ashamed of his family's humble circumstances. He believed he deserved better, and made no secret of his feelings.

"I remember Anna saying nothing was ever good enough for her brother", a family friend told me once. "She said that while the rest of the Ross children accepted their parents weren't well-off and wore hand-me-downs without complaining, Finbarr refused. He said he wouldn't be seen dead in such clothes - so his mother bought him new ones. He was cossetted by Eileen, and still is. To this day she won't hear a word against him."

Most small boys dream about being footballers or train-drivers when they grow up, but for young Finbarr it was visions of wealth and social status that sent him off to sleep at night. Far away from Dunmanway, on the other side of the world it seemed, there was a great city called Dublin where the rich and powerful lived. To Finbarr, its Georgian streets might well have been paved with gold, such was its magic. One day, he vowed, he'd get to Dublin, whatever it took him to do it. And when he arrived he'd eat at the best restaurants, be seen at the best parties; he'd become part of the select circle of people who led charmed lives.

By his early teens, Finbarr Ross he had become a self-taught expert on how the other half lived, and knew all about their custom of sending their sons to expensive boarding-schools for secondary education. He naturally expected Nathaniel and Eileen to do the same for him.

But there was one problem. The Rosses could hardly afford to keep their seven children fed and clothed, let alone pay first-class school fees for their social-climbing eldest son. They told him they were sorry, but boarding-school was out of the question - they just didn't have the money. Finbarr would have to go to a State secondary school like his brothers. To a boy who had already begun to despise his parents for being poor, this was the last straw. He replied furiously that he'd make his own way in the world, without their help. He'd be a success. He'd show them.

In 1959, at the age of 14, Finbarr left full-time education forever and took his first job as an assistant at Atkinson's hardware store on the main street. A few months later, without so much as a by-your-leave, he walked out of the job, the family home and Dunmanway. Where did he go? Just forty miles north, to lodgings in Mallow and a job in another hardware shop. But it was a start.

The pattern of his working life so far had followed that of countless young Irishmen in the '50s and '60s who left school with no qualifications at 14 - taking poorly-paid jobs with no prospects save growing old behind a counter in a dead-end town. It was either that or joining the annual flood of emigrants to Britain in search of soul-destroying work on a building site. Don't talk to me about the luck of the Irish.

But Finbarr knew this stage of his life was only temporary. He had many years ahead of him and his natural charm to exploit. Weighing out nails for customers in the hardware shop, his glance would stray to the door. Beyond that door was the sky, and as far as he was concerned that sky was the limit.

At the age of 16, he left his native Cork for good. You'd think he'd have retained some kind of affection for the place where he spent his childhood, but when in late 1991 a reporter asked him about his birthplace, his reply was dismissive: "I was born in a small town in Cork. I got out as soon as I could and moved to Dublin."

1961 was the year that saw Finbarr Ross begin to fulfil his boyhood ambitions. He packed up his belongings and, leaving his family behind with hardly a thought, headed north. What was going through the fledgling fraudster's mind as his train sped towards Dublin? I can only speculate, but I'll bet the word 'money' was in there somewhere.

It was soon after his arrival in Dublin that the process began which, according to family sources, was to turn Finbarr Ross into the kind of man he is today. The story of his conversion from lowly farmer's son to high-living swindler is a singular one.

For a boy growing up in rural Ireland in the 50s and 60s, the central figure in the community was the local priest. He was the man you looked up to and feared, the man who had the power to save you from the torments of Satan - they still preached hellfire and brimstone in those days - and the man responsible for deciding which were acceptable codes of conduct. The priest wielded the power in a small town; he saw all and knew all. I can well remember as a kid the ritual of the confession, racking my brains to think of sins to admit to and be absolved from. And when Father paid a visit to the family home, out came the best tea-service.

So if a priest took a personal interest in a young man's welfare, it's fair to say he would be hugely flattered. If you were singled out from the flock for special attention by Father, you were destined for great things. You might even end up being called to the priesthood yourself - the dream of many a proud Irish parent.

In a suburb of Dublin there lived a priest who had always taken an interest in the welfare of young people. When, in 1961, he met the raw young Finbarr Ross, newly up from the country, he took it upon himself to teach this boy the ways of the big city. He offered Finbarr free board and lodging, and set about smoothing off the rough edges.

It's fair to say the priest became Finbarr's mentor. He had many friends in high places, and wasted no time in introducing his impressionable young protegé to them. Men at the highest levels of Church and State were charmed by this handsome lad with the broad Cork accent. At first, he seemed easily manipulated - his new found friends could wrap him round their little fingers. But soon he learned how to take advantage of them.

The man of the cloth and the boy from the farm lived under the same roof for five years, until Finbarr was 21. You'd think a teenager taken on by a priest would grow up a humble, God-fearing member of society. But not Finbarr Ross.

At the age of 21, Ross left his priest behind and took digs in Rathgar. He was forced to go back to work to keep himself fed, and found a job doing the one thing he knew - serving in a hardware shop, Baxendales of Capel Street. Weighing out nails in Dublin, he may have consoled himself, was at least a step up from weighing out nails in Cork.

But then came a welcome distraction. Up to now, women seemed to have eluded Ross; he had never had a girlfriend. But while serving on the Baxendales stand at the 1968 Spring Show, he fell in love.

Next to the hardware shop's stand was one displaying riding tackle. Ross accidentally knocked a saddle off it, tripping up a passing girl. From her less than dignified position sprawled on the ground, 17 year-old Bernadette looked up at the handsome, profusely apologetic Corkman and knew that here was the man of her dreams. She had fallen for him in both senses.

Her feelings were reciprocated. The girl who lay at the young man's feet that April day at the RDS was a real beauty. Bernadette was, in fact, modelling at the Spring Show that year.

The pair became inseparable, and soon Ross was taken home to Monaghan to meet the family. According to a friend, Bernadette's middle-class parents were bowled over by the charm and good looks of this young man with the broad Cork accent - an accent he was already working on losing. (These days, the only time he lapses back into his natural brogue is when the drink's in him.) The lovers became engaged, and for a while everything in the garden was rosy. And although Ross didn't know it, his wife-to-be's contacts would in the future prove indispensable in his climb up the business ladder.

The couple were married in Carrickmacross on February 15, 1969. Ross bid a final farewell to the hardware trade, and moved a step closer to the world he yearned to be part of when he took a job with one of Ireland's fastest-growing companies. Roadstone was a quarrying concern which reflected the changing face of the country's economy at that time. After years of blinkered economic policies, we were now welcoming foreign investment. This, plus ambitious Government programmes, encouraged the development of go-ahead operations such as Roadstone.

By the time Ross had arrived in Dublin, there was a whole new world of commercial wealth, oiled by political influence, which was wide open for exploitation by anyone bold enough and with the right contacts. As we now know, this was the start of the notorious "golden circle" of politicians and businessmen lining each other's pockets for personal gain which would culminate in the 1991 summer of scandals.

But in the late '60s, all this stroke-pulling seemed new and exciting. Ross built up his contacts (some of the people he'd met in his five-year sojourn with the priest now began to prove useful), watched, and waited. He began to be noticed; people started talking about this up-and-coming young man with the gift of the blarney. Soon, the mighty Norwich Union insurance company offered him a job with a three-year contract in the South of England.

And so Ross and his new bride Bernadette took the well-worn emigrant trail. But unlike so many before him, he would never have to dirty his hands on a building site.

The couple rented a house in the London dormitory town of Shenfield in Essex, and Ross started work at the Norwich Union's branch in nearby Ilford. The next three years were to prove an invaluable apprenticeship for his forthcoming career as a swindler.

He took to the business as if born to it. His duties included not only ensuring clients were covered by insurance for any eventuality, but also soliciting investments from them. After just a few months, he knew this was how he'd make his fortune. Never much of a drinker up till then, he took to relaxing after work with some of his male colleagues, sinking vodka after vodka in a pub near the office.

It didn't take the ambitious young Corkman long to realise just how easy it was to encourage people to sink their money into what were often misleadingly called "securities". Let's face it, if we all share one ambition in life it's to be financially safe and free from worry. So if someone we believe is an expert tells us this or that scheme can't go wrong, that we could double or treble the value of our savings, many of us will tend to put our faith in him and push any doubts aside.

If I've learned one thing about human nature in my eight years of fighting for justice for Finbarr Ross's victims, it's that the promise of money turns the wisest of us into fools. We put our judgement on hold and believe what we want to believe. Back in 1969, it took the charming young Norwich Union broker no time at all to pick up on this weakness.

Ross learned how easy it is to solicit investments from individuals with a bit of capital put by. He learned how money, once invested, becomes little more than figures on an account-sheet which appear, disappear and then reappear with extra figures added on. It was all so easy. Most importantly, he learned that you could get cash out of people for little more than a promise - and the bigger the amounts involved, the bigger the cut for the broker.

Then came a tragedy that, according to people who know Finbarr Ross well, changed him totally and irrevocably.

Ross and his wife had been trying for a child since the start of their marriage, but there were difficulties - Bernadette had suffered TB as a girl, and had been warned motherhood might be risky. But she was determined; she wanted a baby. And so did her husband. More than anything; more than even money, perhaps.

Their dream came true in July 1971, when Bernadette gave birth to a son, Bryan. But the couple's joy was short-lived. The baby died after just four days.

Bernadette mourned her devastating loss quietly and privately, but Finbarr was literally wild with grief. The funeral of their longed-for first child took place at Brentwood, Essex. When Bryan's tiny coffin was lowered into the ground, his sobbing father jumped in after him. Finbarr had to be dragged from the grave by fellow mourners - it was either that or be buried along with his son.

"He was a changed man after that", a friend of the Rosses told me. "Up till then he had always been a bit of a rogue, but was capable of compassion and sentiment. After Bryan's death, all that mattered was money. When it came to people, he just didn't care." According to this friend, Ross was to shout at

Bernadette during an argument some years later: "Don't you understand? I have no feelings."

In the months following the tragedy, Ross immersed himself in his work. After three years with Norwich Union, he decided it was time to put his new-found knowledge to better use. He broke his contract six months before its completion, left the company and set up his own brokerage.

But this first venture out on his own failed for two reasons. The strength of his ambition was leading him to attempt too much too soon and, more importantly, he was missing that ingredient vital to business success - contacts.

Despite having built up quite a client-list in his time with the insurance company, Ross hadn't connected with enough of the 'right' people. The 'old school tie' network was still very much in operation in the South of England, with success often being down to little more than which college you went to or which big-shots your dad or uncle knew. Finbarr, the cute charmer from across the Irish Sea, would never belong to such a world and he knew it.

Finbarr Ross left England with no regrets. Toughened by tragedy, with three years' valuable experience under his belt and the loving Bernadette by his side, the farm-boy returned to his golden city.

• • •

Back in Dublin in 1973, Ross took a job as a broker at Richard Duggan Insurance on St. Stephen's Green. He and Bernadette found the perfect house, a three-bedroom semi in Leixlip, Co. Kildare, half-an-hour's drive from the city centre. But Ross, with his less- than-stable finances (even then, he spent more than he earned), found it impossible to get a mortgage.

In that situation, you and I would probably have rented a house and waited until our circumstances had improved enough to convince the building societies we were a good risk. Not Finbarr Ross. At the age of just 26, he responded to what he saw as a humiliating snub by starting his own building society. (This also solved his mortgage problem.)

The Family Building Society began trading in Dublin at the beginning of

1973, with Ross as Chairman and Managing Director. It didn't take long to grow, thanks to its founder's instinctive feel for the right contacts.

From the beginning, Ross knew that if his new venture was to flourish he'd have to establish close links with the auctioneers. As the people who actually sell homes, they have a huge influence over where the buyers borrow the money to pay for them.

Within a year of opening, the Family Building Society had branches throughout the Republic of Ireland, and the photogenic Finbarr was being hailed on television and in the Press as an exciting new face on the business scene. When the Family Building Society opened its Cork office, a laudatory article in the Examiner described its 26 year-old chairman as **the youthful and dynamic .. Finbarr Ross**, and explained that two of its main selling-points were ... **quick decisions on mortgages and an efficient service. Finbarr says that people lose heavily through paying interest on bridging loans, hence the importance of quick mortgage completions**. Back in the '70s, it seemed Ross had a commendable concern for the financial well-being of his fellow-man. Either that, or he had learned how to make his charm and credibility work even on cynical journalists. The man should have been in politics.

Ross's golden touch, and the resulting change in his financial fortunes, were being reflected in his home life. A second son, Ian, was born, and to his parents' joy survived. In 1974, Ross and Bernadette moved from Leixlip nearer to the centre of things, buying an elegant house in the affluent North Dublin suburb of Castleknock, close to Phoenix Park.

Now truly a man of property, on his rare days off work Ross would take walks in the park and reflect that at last he was making it. Just four years after leaving small-town Cork to seek his fortune, here he was, the boss of a money-spinning business with branches throughout Ireland, married to a beautiful woman and living at one of Dublin's most desirable addresses. Soon he would become a father for the second time. (He and Bernadette would have three children altogether.)

While on these walks, Ross would sometimes spot members of the exclusive All-Ireland Polo Club astride their immaculately turned- out steeds, enjoying their favourite pastime. He would be among them soon, he knew. To him, membership of the club would mean far, far more than the chance of a few chukkas. It would mean acceptance to the charmed circle.

In the meantime, the champagne lifestyle that would become the Finbarr Ross trademark was underway in earnest. Money was no object as he splashed out on fast cars, paintings and meals at top Dublin restaurants. He started buying polo-ponies, often flying first-class to Argentina on impulse to inspect potential purchases. His wife wondered where all this conspicuous wealth was coming from. Bernadette knew Finbarr was making a success of himself, but he couldn't have got that rich that quickly - could he? Bernadette began to worry that they were living beyond their means, but when she questioned her husband about his financial affairs he would go out and get drunk. To this day Bernadette herself refuses to talk about Finbarr or their marriage.

By the mid-70s, storm-clouds were gathering over the Family Building Society. The business, perhaps because of the extravagant spending habits of its boss, was in a bad way. In an attempt to avert collapse, Ross approached one of his contacts, Lord Iveagh, who offered to bail the Society out financially in return for board membership. The co-directors disliked Iveagh, and after a bitter dispute with them Ross resigned, for "health reasons", from the business he had founded. Soon after he left, it was taken over by the Educational Building Society.

For a few months in 1975, Finbarr Ross was unemployed and, by his standards, penniless. This is an experience he pledged he would never tolerate again.

But these temporarily straitened circumstances didn't hold Ross back in business. In late '75 he started a "friendly society" named The Irish Investments Society Ltd. Because of a loophole in Irish law at the time, he was able to collect deposits from the public and use them for his own loans and investments, without a banking licence. This suited Ross down to the ground. He began making regular business trips across the Atlantic, soliciting investments from wealthy Irish-Americans who were only too happy to entrust large sums of money to this charming young financier from the land of their ancestors.

One of IIS's first investors was a Mr. Hussey, and Ross employed his daughter Nuala to work in the office. An extremely capable and eye-catching woman, Nuala Hussey would serve as the only recorded employee of Finbarr's Fairytale Bank - otherwise known as the International Investments North American Fund. If Ross's version of events was to be believed, Ms Hussey was simultaneously in Dublin, the Isle of Man, Gibraltar and Texas. I'm glad I didn't have to pay her travel expenses.

When the convenient legal loophole was closed in 1976, and new legislation required friendly societies to register as banks, Ross knew he would have a difficult job obtaining a licence. He had already attempted to register the Irish Investments Society as a bank in Jersey, the Isle of Man and Gibraltar, and had received the official equivalent of "You must be joking" from each. Just for a while, it seemed Finbarr's activities might be nipped in the bud.

But then along came salvation - in the form, naturally, of a contact. While the Rosses had been living in England, Bernadette had worked for top London solicitor Sir George Bell, teaching his Turkish niece English. Sir George put Ross in touch with a friend of his, prominent Gibraltarian solicitor Guy Stagnetto. Ross's investment company was incorporated on the Rock of Gibraltar on November 12, 1976.

Nineteen months later, the Gibraltar authorities would grant him the banking licence he so badly needed. On June 26, 1978, the Irish Investment Society officially became a bank - only by now it had changed its name to one more in keeping with its new, jet-set image: International Investments.

George Finbarr Ross was ready for business. But he could afford to bide his time, and it would be another three years before he was to pull off one of the boldest and most heartless strokes in Irish business history.

• • •

From the Sunday Independent, October 20, 1991: **In the yellowish light of the Tipperary bar in downtown Dallas, Finbarr Ross has the floor. Experiencing no difficulty in making himself heard above the noise of the**

band - for Mr. Ross has a Cork twang that carries - he looks me straight in the eye and proclaims 'I got where I am today through hard work. In Ireland they don't know the meaning of it. Half the people in Limerick have never done a day's work in their lives.'

Ross's drinking buddies smile indulgently. 'That's our Finbarr!' their smiles read - and I get the impression they've heard this many, many times before.

The clientele of the Tipperary is in two minds about Finbarr Ross. Some love the man; others merely tolerate him. 'He's a bullshitter', one drinker says, 'always on about the polo-ponies he owned in Ireland.'

Nine years before the Sunday Independent's Mark Smith tracked the missing Finbarr Ross down to Dallas, the scheming financier was in his beloved Dublin riding on the crest of a wave, wealthy beyond even his wildest dreams. International Investments was pulling in the deposits, thanks partly to its still-youthful boss's rich and powerful contacts at the All-Ireland Polo Club.

By 1982, Finbarr was up there where he knew he belonged. Not only had he been accepted into the charmed circle of Dublin's privileged polo-playing yuppies, but he was a club official. Serving on the finance sub-committee, no less. (That isn't a joke, I promise you.) Among Finbarr's fellow-officials was another Corkman, Declan Collins, a high-powered chartered accountant with the Government's favourite firm Stokes Kennedy Crowley.

Collins, a close friend of the then Taoiseach, Charles J. Haughey, lived with his wife Vera in the quietly affluent Bullock Harbour area of Dalkey, Co. Dublin. Next door to Collins lived auctioneer Desmond Scales, a close friend of an up-and-coming young Dublin barrister named Colm Allen. Collins and Allen had met socially at several of Desmond Scales' parties.

As for the flamboyant Finbarr, he was by now living with wife number two (out of three), in an apartment above the Dublin head office of International Investments at 27, Leeson Park. This arrangement was only temporary - the couple was waiting to move into Shinrone, the magnificent solar house on twenty acres of land Ross was having built out in Clonee at a cost of nearly

£500,000.

In 1982, the membership list at the All-Ireland Polo Club read like a roll-call of Ireland's top people, featuring names like Lord Charles Beresford, the Earl of Tyrone and Lord Waterford. But of the 32 names on the membership list, to a true social snob it would be those of Ross and Collins that stood out.

Why? Because they were the only members of the All-Ireland Polo Club who hadn't been born into money. Both had been born and raised in Co. Cork; both had made it on their own, by fair means or (in Ross's case) foul. And while this didn't make them the closest friends on this earth, it established a bond between them.

In common with their fellow members, Ross and Collins had sunk money into bloodstock. Their horses were looked after by respected Kilkenny trainer Jim Bolger. Ross, always the optimist, had great expectations of his acquisitions, in particular his mare Beechlawn Flyer, which he considered a sound investment. Sound investments and Finbarr Ross don't really seem to go hand-in-hand - as far as I can establish, 'Beechlawn Flyer' never came close to winning a race.

The two men also shared an interest in politics.

In the early '80s, Declan Collins' firm Stokes Kennedy Crowley (SKC) made millions from liquidations and Government and corporate accounts. Founding partner Laurence Crowley - another Polo Club member - would receive £600,000 in fees from the controversial McCartan liquidation. International companies arriving to do business in Ireland tended to be pointed SKC's way. The firm grew fat on Fianna Fail recommendations, and senior partner Collins was put in charge of the party's fund-raising activities - activities in which his wife Vera joined enthusiastically. Vera would be rewarded for her sterling work on behalf of the party. In 1991 Charles Haughey appointed her to the board of the Abbey Theatre.

Finbarr Ross was also heavily involved in Fianna Fail, and canvassed for Brian Lenihan in the 1977 General Election. However, Ross would support Des O'Malley in his first attempt to displace Charles Haughey as party leader.

Among Ross's fellow O'Malley supporters was solicitor Paul Smithwick, who owned shares in three International Investments subsidiaries - Anchor Properties, Century Investments and Shelmar Holdings - and had acted for Kenansville Ltd., a company owned by Ross with Des O'Malley's cousin Pat. 25, South Frederick Street, where Smithwick had his office, would become the headquarters of the Progressive Democrats.

It is PD leader Des O'Malley, now Minister for Industry and Commerce in Albert Reynolds' coalition government, who is steadfastly refusing to take any action over the £7 million "sting" perpetrated by Finbarr Ross on 1,200 hapless investors between the years 1981 and '84 - a scandal which many people at the highest levels of Ireland's Government and legal and business community would like to see buried.

Ask yourself two questions. How did Ross pull off such an audacious swindle? And, more importantly: How has he managed to escape justice?

For the answers, I would ask you to turn to the next chapter. It begins with that name-change from Irish Investments to International Investments; from a questionable 'friendly society' to an out-and- out fraud.

"There'll be no end to Finbarr's rainbow", a business associate of Ross told me once. "He'll just keep going." Believe me, there are plenty of people in high places delighted to see the charming con- man still chasing that rainbow. And still getting away with it.

Chapter Two

THE STING

There is really no such thing as the perfect scam, but to find it is the dream of every conman who ever lived. The swindler's Unholy Grail; the immaculate crime.

When Finbarr Ross created International Investments, he got about as close to that goal as I've yet seen anyone do. He managed to keep the fraud going for six years - an astonishing achievement. It could have been for far longer, but like so many others before him, he fell into the usual trap of the cheat. He got too greedy.

The sheer scale of his illicit enterprise was formidable. The deeper I dug into the affairs of Ross and IIL the more intrigued I became. And the more obsessive about this case.

There was one thing which was absolutely genuine about International Investments. It was truly international. Like a modern computer hacker let loose on the electronic circuits of someone else's system, he discovered how to tap into an existing network - the vast web of multi-national finance - and use it for his own ends. He wasn't the first, and I shudder when I think that he undoubtedly will not be the last, but Ross certainly secured himself a place in the history of fiscal fraud.

Ross had several cards in his favour. He was financially literate and knew well that his chosen sphere of operations, offshore banking, was riddled like a sieve with legal loopholes. He took the trouble to get to know them well. Ross also knew one other essential ingredient, about human nature and its infinite capacity for moral weakness. He realised that, like himself, all the world is out to make a fast buck. Everyone wants more money.

Ross played that trump card for all it was worth. He used it to offer incentives to gullible investors, incentives which weren't illegal but were redolent with the promise of easy money. No tax payments and the best interest rates around. Everybody's dream.

He played the same game with certain of his allies and his influential friends. They too found themselves the recipients of Ross' benevolence, and in return they helped him along his way.

He used that card again with the brokers who threw him business in return for his high commissions. Human weakness. Moral frailty. We all suffer from them, and that's how George Finbarr Ross made a fortune, leaving his victims with nothing.

The short corporate career of International Investments Limited is a familiar story in the Republic of Ireland. We've just got too familiar with scandal and corruption. Every day the papers are full of it; Telecom Eireann and the revelations at the Beef Tribunal; less recently, the Arms Trial and phone-tapping. It's a sorry thing to say, but we've almost grown to accept it. Maybe Finbarr Ross reckoned that everyone in Ireland was so fed up to the back teeth with corporate infamy that his own contributions to the national cesspool would be overlooked; that Gibgate would just fade away over the years and be forgotten.

But I'm not going to let that happen. Even if George Finbarr Ross is still living the high life on his ill-gotten profits in 20 years' time, I'd like you to remember the truth about him. You never know, you might run across him someday.

The case of IIL is different from the normal tales of shady dealing between the politicians and the money-men. And what makes it so different is that we're not dealing here with some grey area of dubious morality, wallowing in the murk between angelic white and satanic black. This case is cut and dried. Ross didn't just bend the regulations a bit; he broke all the rules.

The sorry story of the rise and fall of IIL took me years to piece together. For a long time, many of the pieces of the jigsaw didn't seem to fit. IIL was a many-tentacled monster, and getting to the heart of it was the toughest test of staying power I've ever encountered. Gibgate has cost me dear, and not just in financial terms.

I've stuck with this case ever since one distraught investor, Frank Kelly, telephoned to ask for my help. That was back on May 26, 1984, just before the liquidators were called into IIL. I didn't want to take it on, but in the end I just couldn't say no. Kelly kept ringing me back all day, and the more I told him to get lost, the more persistent he became.

I'm not in the habit of leaving cases unsolved, and that's the way it's going to be with Gibgate. I've been labelled a few things for staying the course; people have called me a madman, an obsessive. Circulars have been sent around warning people that I'm a liar and a cheat. But when all that's said and done, there are hundreds of ruined people who still see me as their only hope, and I've no intention of letting them down.

Gibgate is different. You can forget all the "inside stories" of frauds and swindles, written by journalists with an eye for the sensational or politicians being, in the words of a British Attorney General, "economical with the truth". This one's written by me, a private investigator, and I was there.

There's no great mystique about being a private eye; you don't develop X-ray eyes or telepathy. But it does have one great advantage. There are no constraints holding you back, no subtle power-plays swinging you this way or that. I don't have to bear in mind what my readers want, as a journalist might. I don't have to woo the voters like a politician. I can just tell it to you straight.

And anyway, there's no need to dramatise things - the story of International Investments is sensational enough as it stands.

• • •

This, then, is the diary of a fraud.

International Investments was officially born on June 26, 1978, the date Finbarr Ross was granted a banking licence by the Gibraltar authorities. Its main office was named as 186, Main Street, Gibraltar. The real story lay elsewhere.

Why did George Finbarr Ross choose Gibraltar as the official base of his operations? The answer is found by examining some of the myriad loopholes in Irish and international financial law. Ross's original company, the Irish Investments Society Limited, came under the jurisdiction of the Republic's Industrial and Provident Societies Act. Its owner didn't suffer from the usual banking regulations for the very reason that IIS did not have the word 'bank' in its name. Ross was able to operate freely, collecting deposits from the public and using them to make loans and investments. He had no need of an Irish banking licence.

But the authorities were rightly becoming concerned about the way this act was being abused, and in particular the very loophole that Ross was so successfully exploiting with IIS. He wasn't alone in twisting the weaknesses of the law to his own advantage; others were finding out that anyone could play at being a banker.

So the Dail introduced new legislation under the Industrial and Provident Societies (Amendment) Act, which would have effectively put an end to Ross's surrogate banking. The new rules meant that he would have either to register as an official bank or re-finance his borrowings from an established bank rather than from members of the public. That would turn the whole thing into a legally constrained operation, hardly Ross's sort of thing at all, and would open up IIS to close scrutiny by the authorities.

Ross took professional advice. He discovered the advantages of offshore banking - registering as a bona fide foreign bank, thus avoiding the pitfalls of proper control in this country.

He then went loophole shopping. Foreign rules and regulations give vastly different measures of legal control, and Ross wanted to find the one with the least restraints on his activities, present and future. After long deliberation, he chose Gibraltar

The tiny colony which guards the only entrance at the west of the Mediterranean Sea has had a stormy past. Centuries of invasion; centuries of war. The British conquered the Rock in 1704, and quickly realised its strategic importance. They hung on to it, and it seemed a mutually agreeable situation; in 1967 the islanders held a referendum and voted to remain British. Two years later they were rewarded for their loyalty with their own Constitution and responsibility for the island's internal government.

Since then, the island's financial affairs have boomed. A huge market of investors was discovered among the English expatriates living along the Costa del Sol in Spain, and with the Rock's own anglophone residents. As more people arrived on this Mediterranean tax haven, so the demand grew for a varied array of financial and investment services.

It soon became widely known among Britons that the best way of avoiding tax on their dream retirement home, a Spanish villa or apartment, was to buy it through a Gibraltar registered company. The financial sector's support groups, the accountants and solicitors, immediately flourished.

Ross was told that Gibraltar was a good bet for his new company. He wouldn't actually have to live there; there was no need to encounter a single Barbary ape. All he had to do was have a registered office on the island. Ross approached his family contact, prominent Gibraltarian solicitor Guy Stagnetto, and enquired about obtaining the relevant documentation.

The Irish Investments Society was enrolled on the Gibraltar Companies Register on November 12, 1976. In June 1978, Gibraltar's authorities granted Finbarr Ross a banking licence, allowing the company, now called International Investments Ltd., to raise deposits from the public. Several conditions were attached. Not less than 90 percent of the total deposits Ross received would have to be kept in a Gibraltarian bank approved by the island's Financial and Development Secretary. Any other deposits were to be placed in a registered bank in Jersey. The funds were to be used for no other purposes than repaying depositors, investment, and loans to residents in the Republic of Ireland.

IIL was also granted tax exemption status in Gibraltar, under the island's Companies (Taxation and Concessions) Ordinance, provided it did not trade inside the island itself. As long as no resident Gibraltarians were making money out of the company it would only have to pay a token annual tax of £225. For Ross this was akin to paying for a meal in a posh Dublin restaurant. This tax-haven status would enable him to dangle the bait of tax-free income in front of hundreds of potential victims back in Ireland.

As far as this point it was fairly simple to follow the evolution of IIL. But then Finbarr Ross added his own special touch to the affair. He set up a maze.

The shares of IIL were held by another Gibraltar tax exempt company named Egret Investment Company Limited. The shares of that company were held by Stagg Nominees Limited, a trustee company owned by the lawyer Guy Stagnetto. The deeper I delved, the more dense Ross's corporate fog became.

During 1978 IIL began the process of taking everything over from the Irish Investment Society. In 1976 the deposits in Ross's original company were £385,151; by the middle of 1978 that figure was down to zero. IIS was dead, and IIL was poised and ready on the starting blocks.

When IIL's first liquidator, Timothy Revill, investigated this transfer of funds, he reported that it seemed to have been carried out with the full agreement of all the IIS investors. He was told they were informed in writing in advance of the transfer, although he admitted he was unable to find any actual record of this crucial letter.

I found that hard to believe. A part of Finbarr Ross's operation which was done according to the book? It was a rare day indeed when Ross did something honest. I asked around, and sure enough I found one investor with IIS, Joseph Coughlan, an old school friend of Ross, who had good reason to join me in this disbelief.

Joe swore an affidavit, saying someone had forged his signature on a document agreeing to the funds being moved. Even Ross's old friends - those who were no longer part of his new, exalted social circle - weren't safe from the all-consuming trickery.

So Finbarr Ross had his dream, his very own bank. IIL was registered in Gibraltar, a fact which has since been used as an excuse by the Irish authorities for taking no action against this swindler. But I discovered that, like so many "facts" in this case, the truth was a very different matter.

IIL was actually being run from Dublin. Its first office was at Fadebrook House, 3, Fade Street, Dublin. But IIL soon moved to its real headquarters at 27, Leeson Park, a leafy street of elegant buildings in the upmarket suburb of Ranelagh. Walk down Leeson Park and you get the same impression that Ross's potential clients and investors must have had. It is an avenue of respectability; a few embassies, a nursing home, some company headquarters with only discreet brass plaques announcing their existence. A very model of solidity. Leeson Park must have lulled many a hapless client into a false sense of security.

In reality, Ross was running IIL as an Irish bank. He was operating out of

Dublin, and the fact that his empire was registered elsewhere was just so much red tape in the records. Unfortunately, Dublin's political and judicial elite still don't see it that way.

Now let me introduce a few of the characters you'll be meeting in the book; the cast list of International Investments Limited.

The directors in those first few years were a mixed bunch. For the sake of record I'll name them here, but some don't play a major part in the unfolding story, so I'll concentrate in a moment on just one.

Lawrie Keighley, a chartered accountant, died in 1979 and was replaced as a director of IIL by his successor in his Gibraltar practice, Michael Morris. Guy Stagnetto we've already met. A third director, a Mr. J. W. V. Cumming, served with IIL between July 3, 1978 and April 2, 1982.

On March 17, 1981 both Mr. Morris and Mr. Stagnetto resigned, and Mr. and Mrs. Ronald Vincent of the Isle of Man were appointed in their place. Which meant that when Mr. Cumming added his resignation to the list in 1982, the Vincents were left as sole directors of this dubious enterprise. Ross's mission was achieved. He and his appointees were now in sole control of the company. There was no longer any need even to pretend the operation was accountable to anyone.

Ronald Vincent was yet another social acquaintance of George Finbarr Ross. When Morris and Stagnetto handed in their resignations Ross knew he had to find somebody to take their place and turned to the Vincents. Would they like to become directors of IIL? Ross used the phrase "offshore directors". Ronald Vincent once described that day. I guess it's the sort of life-shattering decision that would stick in your mind.

"Ross told me that as a director, I would not have any day-to-day responsibility in the affairs of the company. He knew that at this time I was convalescent after a heart attack and was not in a position to assume an active part and responsibility in the management of this or any other company's affairs.

"I naturally assumed from the tenor of the conversation in question that

International Investments Limited was a company owned and controlled by Mr. Ross, and that he was managing the company as a director and was merely looking to me and my wife as non-executive directors.

"At this time, I knew nothing adverse to Mr. Ross and indeed I believed him to be a man of considerable substance and wealth, and of good commercial standing associated with success."

Frank Murray is another character that you'll get to know well as the IIL story unfolds. Murray was a chartered surveyor who shared Ross's office in Leeson Park. But he was much more than that; he was IIL's Chairman. No-one ever elected him to that position, nor was he ever registered as company Chairman of IIL. But to all intents and purposes, Chairman he was.

The way Frank tells the story, you'd think he was an innocent bystander, caught in the crossfire. In an affidavit he swore to Supreme Court of Gibraltar when IIL collapsed, Murray points the finger of blame at Vincent to try and get himself off the hook.

Mr. Vincent (claimed Murray) **was the Managing Director of International Investments Limited and signed the last audited figures of that company in 1982. He and the first named defendant (Ross) ran International Investments, meeting to my knowledge in London, the Isle of Man and Dublin with great regularity ...**

My firm occupied the same premises as Mr. Ross but our businesses were at all times entirely separate and unconnected. At no time was I a director or a shareholder or involved in the running or management of International Investments Limited, nor did I issue any instructions in relation thereto ...

I believe that some confusion may have arisen as to the role of me ... because I signed the bank mandate for its account. The circumstances in which this came to pass were: The first named defendant (Ross), with whom I enjoyed a personal as well as business relationship, was out of the country a good deal of the time. He asked me as an obligement to him to

become a signatory on the bank account in question. This I did.

I was presented from time to time with books of cheques which I signed on request. These cheques were blank when I signed them and I would have been unaware of the purposes for which they were required or the amounts in which they were subsequently issued.

Poor Frank Murray. A luckless stooge? Perhaps he should have taken more care what he signed. Like when he signed his name as "Chairman" of IIL on 7 October 1983.

There's another player in this story whose name will crop up from time to time. Oliver Conlon, Ross's solicitor, and a man who played an active part in the company. Conlon was also a member of that Polo Club elite.

Let's be in no doubt about the role of this gentleman in the dealings of IIL. To make matters perfectly fair I'll quote you a few lines from the report of Timothy Revill, IIL's first liquidator.

... Oliver Conlon, a solicitor who was heavily involved in many of the property transactions financed by International and who himself received personal loans from International. I have not, so far, received from Conlon any account of International's funds handled by him, despite having formally requested a summary of all entries in his client's account relating to International.

The maze got yet more complicated as Ross set up his scam. International Investments ran its funds through several bank accounts; at Ulster Bank branches in Baggot Street, Dublin and in Newry; at the Northern Ireland United Dominions Trust in Dublin; the Allied Irish Finance Company, and Barclays Bank in St Helier, Jersey.

And yes, I almost forgot. They did have a bank account with Barclays International in Gibraltar, too. That was where the deposits were supposed to go; it didn't see much action.

IIL also continued to use bank accounts in the name of the Irish

Investment Society Limited, even though the Registrar of Friendly Societies in Dublin had been assured by Ross that the company's affairs had been wound down. That ploy was to solve a particular problem. Where deposits came in from investors in the Republic and were therefore subject to exchange controls, it was extremely useful for Ross to be able to turn the cash around in an account handling Irish pounds, and re-invest them in the Republic, thus neatly avoiding the need for exchange control permission.

The initial signatories on both IIL and IIS accounts were generally Ross, Murray, and some of their respective secretaries. Some accounts only needed Ross's name on the cheque.

There's a copy still around of a submission by IIL to its main bank. It's an interesting document, and one that Frank Murray must bitterly regret. It purports to be a resolution of a meeting of the Board of Directors of the company held on October 7, 1983. That imaginary meeting authorised Ross, Murray and Patricia Kidney as signatories of cheques. It's certified true by the signatures of Ross, as company secretary, and Murray as Chairman. Once again, the unmistakable autograph of the man who says he knew nothing. Neither man was actually ever elected or registered to those posts.

Ross and Murray set about covering their tracks and hiding their activities from public scrutiny. They did this by using "front" companies, with names which no-one would link to International Investments. Neither the investors themselves nor the authorities would connect this complex of companies with IIL. It took a great deal of searching and cross-referencing to spot the connection between them - the same small band of names cropping up time and again in the web of investment companies, holding companies and development companies.

There were at least six front companies which Ross used. There may be more; I confess Ross's aptitude at corporate juggling may outweigh my skills at spotting his traces.

There was Anchor Properties Limited, with shareholders Paul Smithwick - a founder-member of the Progressive Democrats - and Frank Murray holding the share capital of 100 between them. The directors were Ronald

Vincent and Frank Murray (and originally Smithwick, who resigned on 16 November 1982). Anchor was a property development company.

Kenansville Limited is another organisation with a less than impressive share capital - this time just 2. The link here was the company's solicitor, Paul Smithwick.

Shelmar (Investments) Limited - again with a 2 share capital - had Smithwick as one of the shareholders. Smithwick and Frank Murray were the directors. Shelmar (Holdings) Limited had much the same line-up.

Paul Smithwick's name cropped up again as both shareholder and director of Centenary Investments Limited, and Frank Murray was the manager of a development for Davesco Limited.

In case you are still in any doubt as to what these companies were really set up for, let me quote to you from the affidavit of Timothy Revill sworn in July 1984:

It is to my belief that the Company (IIL) is entitled beneficially to, whether directly or indirectly, equity ownership in the following companies in the amounts stated:

Anchor Properties Limited	**100%**
Kenansville Limited	**100%**
Shelmar (Investments) Limited	**100%**
Shelmar (Holdings) Limited	**100%**
Centenary Investments Limited	**100%**
Davesco Limited	**100%**

It is my belief that the first named Defendant (George Finbarr Ross) has so carried on the affairs of the Company and its investments so as to conceal the true identity of the ownership of all the assets of the Company, including the above mentioned Companies, so as such assets are not available for the benefit of the Company and ultimately the benefit of the depositors. It appears to me that he has used the Company's monies collected

from depositors for his own benefit without acknowledging the true title of the Company to such assets.

In plain, non-legal language, Ross was ripping off all those investors who put their trust in him by diverting money out of IIL and into his own pockets. Let's take a look at a few examples of how he did it.

Ross had never been a man who thought business and scruples should ever go hand in hand. During the time he was running the Irish Investments Society, he took a few, relatively minor excursions into fraud. He loaned investments given to IIS to himself, without the approval of the Board of Directors. He never repaid them. Again without corporate approval IIS loaned £49,000 to a company named Shenfield Management Ltd. Ross controlled that one, too. He also used funds from the company to buy his own art collection, antique bank notes, Krugerrands and antiques, as well as those all-important polo ponies.

Ross bought an apartment at Estepona in Spain. As far as I'm aware he's still legally free to enjoy the odd visit to this extra home on the Costa Del Sol (nowadays often nicknamed the Costa del Crime by the tabloids). Oliver Conlon has since claimed a fifty percent share in the ownership of that property.

But the way Ross dipped his hands into the IIS till was mere child's play compared to the large-scale fraud that was to come. My investigations took a while, but I managed to pinpoint quite a few proven examples. These are not fanciful suppositions, but cases of blatant fraud backed up by strong evidence. I've got all the paperwork, every bit of documentation for each claim I make. Try contrasting that with some of accusations laid at my door by other characters in this IIL story.

• • •

Ross used International Investments funds to buy polo ponies from Argentina. He fraudulently transferred investors' money to his personal accounts at the Bank of Ireland in New York and Allied Irish Bank branches in New York and London. He fraudulently used the company funds to buy shares in Atlantic Resources and Independent Newspapers. Ross got his foothold - and it was a considerable one - into real estate in Houston, Texas through the same source.

When anyone shrugs their shoulders and suggests the money's all gone, that it never existed, I just direct them to Texas. There, in property, oil wells and investment businesses, is the vast majority of the hard-earned cash given to Ross by 1,200 investors. And thanks to certain of his influential friends, he has managed - for the time being - to hang on to it.

Ross wasn't the only IIL luminary on the fiddle. Frank Murray, again describing himself as Chairman of the company, approved several loans to himself and others via the Ulster Bank in Newry. Not one of them has ever been repaid.

Shinrone, Ross's solar-powered dreamhouse and bloodstock stud farm in Co. Meath, benefited from substantial re-direction of IIL funds. He dipped into the cash box to pay sweeteners to brokers from the North who put business his way, and slipped money to a journalist in return for a bit of free public relations hype in the Irish newspapers.

Naturally, Ross wanted to share his good fortune with his friends, so IIL funds were contributed to the Irish Polo Club.

Everyone had a field day; cash was raining down from the heavens. Everyone, that is, except the investors. Those who were due interest were paid back from the deposits of new clients. Their original cash had long since been swallowed up in Ross's corporate quicksands.

Now, I freely admit that some of the more complicated intricacies of offshore financing aren't really something I've had that much to do with in the past. So for some of the legwork - these days it's done on computers, faxes and phones - I enlisted the help of a colleague, a real expert in the field of offshore banking. He had a snoop round Ross's operation abroad, and discovered the terms of that original Gibraltar banking licence had been broken 27 times. On top of that, from 1983 to 1984, when Ross and Murray were still soliciting investments, they actually had no banking licence.

But even Ross's fertile imagination and manipulation couldn't disguise the truth for ever. By the second half of 1983 his nest was well-feathered. Funds from IIL had been swapped to his personal bank accounts and he was already a name to be reckoned with on the Texas real estate scene. He had moved into the oil business, too.

Perhaps Ross saw himself as the J.R. Ewing of County Cork. Just like that notorious dirty dealer and backstabber from the TV series Dallas, he had a few tricks up his sleeve to get the money flowing when the oil dried up. When a well struck the "black gold", it was Ross's well, and the champagne flowed. When the drill bits hit nothing but barren sand, then the well belonged to the unfortunate investors of International Investments. It was a classic case of "heads he wins - tails they lose".

Ross was certainly financially secure, but he had earned that security at a price. IIL now had so many investors that his early policy of paying off the interest by soliciting new custom wasn't keeping pace with the money he owed to existing clients of the company. It wasn't that the money was running out - not Ross's personal fortune - but let's just say the company cash float was almost empty. International Investments had the cash flow problem, not Ross.

That was when Ross's past generosities to the brokers really paid off. (I'll be taking a closer look at this particular breed of financial vampire in the next chapter. They're important, because without them Ross would have had a hard job finding investors in the first place.)

The brokers, spurred on by anxious clients who had not received their interest cheques, were growing restless and suspicious that all might not be well in the headquarters of International Investments. Ross managed to allay their fears for a while, initially by a mass party and brokers' meeting at the Stormont Hotel in Belfast in December 1983. Here his brash confidence actually succeeded in bringing in more funds, rather than what the brokers should have called for - an immediate investigation by the authorities.

But, despite all his efforts, the world was closing in on Ross. That Stormont

Hotel party was the last time he was seen in Ireland. He left for America while IIL collapsed around him. Looking back, I can only assume he'd planned it that way all along.

• • •

In January 1984 a group of brokers from the North, once again under pressure from their investors, formed a delegation and went to visit Frank Murray and Ronald Vincent at 27, Leeson Park. Murray told them there was a deficit of 6.2 million in the IIL accounts. The reason, he explained, was that the vast bulk of that money was invested in the United States. It was invested privately in Ross's name. Murray admitted Ross was not actually a director of IIL.

The brokers put their heads together and hurriedly nominated Ross as a director of the company. They then took Murray and Vincent with them and flew to Texas to meet the man himself.

Ross was accommodating to a degree which surprised them. He agreed that all the investments in the States, the investments made personally by him in his own name, were actually the property of IIL, and wholly the property of IIL. The deputation returned home happy, believing they had secured their clients' money, and agreeing to make Ross a consultant for IIL, on a salary of £3,000 a month. Plus expenses, of course. What the brokers didn't know was that, from all the millions invested by their clients, all but £5,000 had been hidden away in Ross's financial maze.

Ross never came back to Ireland. Vincent, Murray and the brokers took over effective control of International Investments. They met again at Leeson Park, where the enormity of the situation began to sink in. Here they were, in control of a company with debts of £6.2 million. Although Ross had agreed the American investments were IIL's property, it would take at least a year to realise those assets. They faced a catastrophic cash flow problem. Investors were now threatening legal action to get back their money. The new controllers of IIL had none to give them. But despite its imminent collapse, between January and April 1984 IIL continued to receive new deposits from investors.

Ronald Vincent, the man who claimed he'd been taken on as an "offshore director" with a brief to do precisely nothing, was now deeply trapped in the quagmire. He decided to throw in some complications of his own to buy a little breathing space.

Vincent sent a circular to IIL investors, pointing out the company's financial difficulties and asking them to convert their deposits into shares. I'll go into that in more detail in the next chapter; suffice to say here that it would have been folly had they acted on his recommendation. They would become effective owners of IIL themselves, and would have no claim against Ross and his pals once the bank collapsed. Vincent was promising that despite the short term problems, IIL had assets worth "in the region of £4 million". Imminent events would bring the validity of this claim into question.

Then Vincent did something which really demonstrated his appointment as an "offshore director" had been truly warranted. He attempted to transfer the whole operation of International Investments to the Isle of Man, another island tax haven.

Gibraltar had become a far less attractive proposition. The island which first granted George Finbarr Ross his coveted banking licence on June 26, 1978 had toughened things up a little. IIL had been allowed to operate as a bank from 1978 to '82, four years in which they produced not a single set of audited accounts. The only financial record of this fine Gibraltarian company was a solitary balance sheet, prepared in June 1982, when International Investments had been forced to apply for a new banking licence under revised legislation.

The Isle of Man seemed worth a try, albeit a last-ditch attempt to ward off bankruptcy and possible prosecution. If successful, IIL could be re-launched as a solvent company. Besides, Ronald Vincent was himself a Manxman, from the island's capital, Douglas. He would have none of the usual problems of finding accommodation and office space.

International Investments had already used the Isle of Man's financial facilities to filter some of the depositors' money. A considerable slice of the company's funds was invested in portfolio stocks and shares through a company called Meldgate Investments, based on the island. Meldgate's shares were registered in the name of nominees, despite the fact that £263,195 of IIL money was transferred to the company.

Meldgate originally acted as what's called a 'sterling deposit holder' - my apologies for all this financial jargon, but there's really no way to avoid it. This simply meant that it provided security, on a sort of back-to-back basis, to several Irish subsidiaries for loans in Irish pounds. One of the outlets Meldgate chose for investment was Ohio Resources Incorporated, a Canadian oil exploration company, within which Ross had a personal connection. That's offshore banking for you - it's a small world when Finbarr Ross has anything to do with it.

When Ross had obtained his original banking licence in Gibraltar there had been few checks made on his proffered credentials. References were taken, and a call was made to the Bank of England to see if it held a view on International Investments, but even the Gibraltar authorities now admit those scrutinies were far from satisfactory. Brian Traynor, the Gibraltar Banking Commissioner, has publicly said the checks made on George Finbarr Ross were "not adequate".

IIL now had no banking licence to work with, which didn't seem to stop it carrying on as normal. Ronald Vincent was to find out, however, that his planned re-launch on the Isle of Man would meet an entirely different response.

Vincent moved IIL to the Isle of Man from Dublin at the end of February, 1984. But the first the island's banking authorities heard about it was when his letter to IIL's investors, asking them to convert their deposits into shares, went out from a Manx address. The alarm bells began to ring, and IIL was ordered off the Isle of Man within three weeks of Vincent's arrival. A senior Manx banking official told a British Daily Telegraph reporter who looked into the story: "We have quite enough problems of our own. It seems a little unkind of people to come here just to collapse." The Isle of Man was getting exasperated with its increasing notoriety as an "elephant's graveyard", to which companies limped at the end of their days to die.

Death was exactly what was happening to International Investments. When the brokers' cartel, along with Murray and Vincent, tried to get a new bank mandate from IIL's account at the Ulster Bank in Newry, the bank had closed the account. It now realised the company had been run in a fraudulent manner for the past three years, and that all withdrawals and transactions had been illegal.

With only £5,000 left in the IIL bank accounts at the end of May 1984, Vincent went to the authorities in Gibraltar and asked Timothy Revill, a former Isle of Man acquaintance, to go over the books.

The accounts were in a terrible state. IIL's Gibraltar office turned out to be one ramshackle room on Main Street. "I spent four days looking at the books," Revill remembers, "and found them in a hell of a mess. I said the company should go into liquidation."

On June 12, 1984, IIL's shareholders passed a resolution that the company be wound up. A week later, the Supreme Court of Gibraltar appointed Timothy Revill provisional liquidator.

The bubble had burst. International Investments owed its investors £7.3 million.

Some people claim that money is long gone, that Ross's wild extravagance blew the lot on a six-year spending spree. But the truth is different. The money's still there all right, all neatly hidden in American companies - Ross's fraudulent fortune.

And, thanks to his friends in high places, it looks like he gets to keep it.

Chapter Three

"SOMEONE STOLE MY MONEY ..."

What do you think when you open the paper and read that an investor has fallen on hard times? If you're like most of us, you probably imagine some wealthy swank, a "name" with Lloyds of London perhaps, who's down to his last million and has to sell off the Rolls-Royce. You'd have to be an extraordinarily compassionate person to cry into your pint over a story like that.

I'd like to introduce you to John McHale. John's no high-flying money man, but a hard-grafting builder. He's in his late 60s now, and he too knows what it's like to fall on hard times. He was stung by International Investments.

John McHale is a Mayo man, born and raised in Kiltimagh. That town gave us the good-natured insult "culchie", used by Dubliners to take the rise out of country folk. John knew only too well what the city slickers meant. The Kiltimagh of his youth was a place where the only way to get on in life was to leave town. Kiltimagh had no work and no prospects. Like so many before and since, John had little option but to emigrate.

John's story is one I know well. I've heard it a thousand times from clients at the clinics I hold in the Irish Centre in London's Camden Town. The ship to England; the search for work; the endless back-breaking hours on a hundred different building sites. Cheap Irish labour. Where would England be without us?

John worked the sites for 31 years, suffering the normal inventory of injuries which that brutal trade involves. He married Mary, and the couple moved into a small home in Sheringham Avenue in London's Manor Park. Sheringham Avenue is not the poshest street in London town, but the McHales made sure their house was kept neat and tidy. Mary developed a passion for gardening, and grew justly proud of her immaculate lawns and borders.

When life's been hard and you haven't had the lucky breaks, you need a dream to hang on to, and John and Mary McHale were no exception. John had always longed to return home, back to Kiltimagh in County

Mayo. In his long years of toil in the construction trade he managed to save £22,000. It would have been more, enough to buy that little cottage of his dreams back in Ireland, but a spate of injuries dried up his earnings for a while, and John couldn't quite raise the asking price.

Finbarr Ross offered John his dream, and then snatched it back from his grasp.

The McHales reckoned they needed £30,000 to move back to Kiltimagh, and decided the only way to get those extra thousands was to invest the money somewhere it would grow rapidly. John took the plunge and gave his life savings to Kevin Logue of Irish Assets Managements, a United Kingdom subsidiary of International Investments Limited. Logue sought business through personal contacts and with an advertisement placed in the Irish Post, the newspaper for the Irish community in England.

John McHale was satisfied he had made the right decision. A year after his retirement, in June 1984, he would be able to withdraw the money, and his dream would become reality.

Like I say, not all investors are wealthy tycoons swanning around the world on their yachts. Anyone with a bit of cash saved up can try and make it grow in that mysterious world of high finance. Across the water in England advertisements for financial services warn that the value of your savings can go down, as well as up. But with a few notable exceptions, International Investments made sure that their clients' savings simply disappeared.

Finbarr Ross had spent three years with a building society in London, and he knew all about the value of the "small" investor; the middle-aged couple carefully saving for a rainy day; the McHales and a thousand like them, living for their dreams of idyllic retirement. I can't speak for what went through Ross's mind at that time but I would guess he saw his opportunity. Large-scale fraud isn't just about insider trading and crooked boardroom coups. There's money to be made from the real workers, too, if you're not too fussy how you do it.

Kevin Logue also played the middleman for Frank Kelly. Like John McHale, Frank emigrated from Kiltimagh to England to work in construction, but the two never met. Frank laboured on the building sites around Birmingham and settled down there. He had already tried to "make his money work for him", and had invested substantial funds with an Irish building company. The outfit went bust, still owing him the money.

Frank, angry at what he saw as a deliberate con, vowed that this time around he would place his cash wisely. Like John McHale, he reckoned his money was safe as the Rock of Gibraltar with International Investments. A pathetic irony.

Logue was already scoring plenty of successes by convincing Irish emigrants to let him manage their cash. He met Frank Kelly in Birmingham's Anchor Bar. The Anchor was a home from home for the Irish in the area; Tom and Mary Keane, who owned and ran the pub, came from Mayo too.

Everyone agreed Kevin Logue was "a lovely lad", and three of the regulars at the Anchor had already transferred their life savings to him to place with International Investments Limited. Tom and Mary had themselves handed over £81,000. They too dreamed of going home. Mary was 76 and suffering from cancer; she'd had two operations and her speech was seriously impaired.

Mary Keane was enthusiastic about IIL and wanted others to share in her good fortune in discovering the company and the profits it offered. Her sister, Maura Kelly, lived back in Ballintubber Abbey in County Mayo with her husband Jim.

Beware of dreams; they were the one common strand in Finbarr Ross's scam. Everyone has them, and everyone yearns to get something for nothing. Maura and Jim had a dream, too. Maura was the local postmistress, and kept a small grocery store and a bar in need of some pretty drastic renovation. The couple really wanted to start it off again from scratch; rip out the fixtures and fittings and turn the pub into somewhere they could be proud of, a real meeting place for the village.

Maura was embarrassed every summer when relatives and friends dropped in during holiday visits. She had no children, and wanted to see more of her nephews who were living in England. Ideally, she'd love one of them to move to Mayo. The newly renovated pub would be her gift to him to make it happen.

Maura and Jim reckoned it would cost them at least £70,000 to rebuild the bar. Her life savings were only £51,000. Where was she going to get the extra money?

And then, like the final piece slotting into place in some crooked, twisted jigsaw, her sister rang. She told Maura about Finbarr Ross's bank, International Investments Limited.

If she invested the £51,000 for just three years she'd have the money she needed. When I met Maura, she admitted to me she'd not told her husband anything about the investment. She didn't want to worry him.

It's something I see only too often as a private investigator; as soon as someone invests a bit of money it lends credence to the whole venture, and others follow suit. Sometimes it works out fine, and everyone comes out smiling. But the only smile left in this whole sorry IIL affair is the broad, grinning smirk on George Finbarr Ross's suntanned face.

Some of the investors were singled out for special attention; that charmingly deadly Finbarr Ross touch.

The overwhelming majority of IIL's deposits came from Northern Ireland. There was a sound financial reason for this. The Republic of Ireland was at this time subject to currency exchange controls; the North was not.

Ross visited potential large depositors himself, or sent the attractive Nuala Hussey.

Ross didn't know the North, and hired a schoolteacher in Lisburn -

Laurence McDermott - to drive him around to meet likely clients. He told them they would receive 17 percent tax free interest if they put their cash into IIL's North American Fund. Who could fail to be impressed by this smooth-talking businessman with his own Houston office block, glowingly described in the company's brochure?

David and Emily Mairs lived outside Glenarm on the eastern coast of County Antrim. David was a tall, well built man, a six-footer who'd made a success of life. He was a respected retired architect. His house was perfect - a model of tasteful design - with extensive landscaped gardens. He'd obviously used his architectural skills to build himself his own personal Utopia, high above the stormy Antrim coastline.

But the Mairs' retirement wasn't all roses. David, who'd been a very active man, was now confined to a wheelchair after a stroke. And there was more. A number of investments and business ventures had gone disastrously wrong. He was distressed, and would now have to be careful about where he invested his £115,000 nest-egg.

IIL seemed just the ticket, and 17 percent? Well, you wouldn't get 17 percent in any ordinary high street building society, would you?

Nuala Hussey seemed such a charming lady. And Finbarr himself had visited, too, and David Mairs told me many years later he'd summed him up as a gentleman. Yes, he'd had no doubts about the right course to take and invested with IIL. He recommended the company to his sister, too, and she gave that charming gentleman Mr Ross a further £62,000. His two daughters liked the sound of IIL and invested money as well.

David Mairs felt happy and satisfied. After all, he'd just put his whole family on to a surefire business venture, hadn't he? In all, the Mairs family invested more than £200,000 with Finbarr Ross. The bulk of Ross' business came from the North. About 600 investors in Northern Ireland were attracted to IIL, principally on the recommendation of the various brokers. The brokers painted a mouth- watering picture of International Investments; high interest rates, tax-free money, and total secrecy from the Inland Revenue.

Let's face it, none of us is really going to jump for joy at the prospect of handing over large chunks of our hard earned cash to the tax man. This single incentive, more than any other, proved the most effective bait that Ross could dangle.

How much do you reckon you really know about the way high finance operates? It's something I've certainly had a few brushes with over the years, and I freely admit I'm still learning. Virtually all of Ross' investors were financially ignorant. No insult intended there, but it's a sad fact of life that most people are.

It's that ignorance which makes them almost totally reliant on the middlemen, the brokers. How else are you going to handle things if you want to invest a few thousand pounds and need to find out the best place to put it? You could stare at the share prices and unit trust listings in the Irish Times for months and still be none the wiser. Investment is effectively a closed shop for most of us, and we have no other option but to trust the broker when we reckon it's time to make our nest egg work for us.

But the trust involved in any working relationship between client and broker is strictly a one-way affair. The balance of power is completely with the brokers. We've no way of finding out whether they're giving us the best advice. Half the time we don't really have a clue what they're talking about. It's a kind of blind faith, and we have to strike it lucky.

It's easy to imagine that all brokers are honour bound to do their best for us in every conceivable situation. And so they should be, but that's not the way it happens in real life.

Brokers are powerful; their clients, the people with the money, are totally in their hands. The brokers control what happens to the cash, where it goes. Investment companies know that only too well. And sometimes they try to take advantage of it.

It's perfectly normal practise for these companies to offer good commissions to the brokers in order to get their hands on their clients' money. There's nothing at all illegal about that. But sometimes these middlemen are offered a damn sight more than a fair percentage and a glossy brochure to wave at the next person who walks into their office.

I'm talking about what's known in the trade as "sweeteners", little gifts to get the broker on your side. Finbarr Ross proved to be a master of the technique.

Ross went well beyond the normal, unofficial code of practice in luring the brokers. Quite apart from the blatant, barefaced lies he told about IIL and the strength of the company, his methods of soliciting business were from the very beginning immoral, and probably illegal.

In the North, for example, where the bulk of the money came from, IIL paid the investment brokers a four percent commission on any money placed with International Investments. Think about it; that's a handy sum simply for directing someone's money in a certain direction.

But it wasn't just the commission. Ross did things in style. He lavished gifts on the brokers; family holidays, luxury Rolex watches, and heavy bonuses on large investments.

In early October 1983 Ross sent a note to the brokers with offers of yet another special bonus.£500 on top of their normal commission for introducing new business worth more than £150,000. By this time, of course, the brokers were already getting letters from disgruntled investors, complaining they hadn't been getting their interest cheques. But what did the brokers do about it?

They allowed Ross to explain away their clients' worries with bland talk about International Investments' £10 million in the United States. After all, the brokers couldn't lose, could they? It wasn't their cash.

You may be wondering who these brokers are. They're the people about whom one investor, Harry Duffin, after the whole scam was revealed, commented: "I blame Finbarr Ross, but I blame the brokers even more - they're the ones who only live for their commission." Harry invested with IIL on the advice of financial advisor Drew Beckett, who persuaded him to put money into Ross's bank.

Drew Beckett played a starring role in an English Channel 4 TV documentary about the International Investments scandal. The consumer watchdog programme "4 What It's Worth" spoke to both Harry Duffin and another of Beckett's clients, Isobel Hall, who like Harry lost every last penny she invested with IIL.

Reporter Susan Osman, who presented the programme, tracked Beckett down on a shopping trip. Let me quote you that encounter from the official transcript of the documentary.

We have come to find Mrs Hall and Mr Duffin's investment advisor who is Drew Beckett, who works for Liberty Life Assurance in Belfast. We have managed to track him down, he is in one of these shops along here, and in a moment I am going to ask him a few questions. However, he has refused to appear on our programme. In fact he told us he knows very little about International Investments. Then why, if he does not know very much about the company, did he advise Mrs Hall and Mr Duffin to invest their money with International Investments?

"Excuse me, are you Mr Drew Beckett? I am Susan Osman from '4 What Its Worth' and I would like to ask you a few questions. Why did you encourage Mrs Isobel Hall to invest in International Investments? Excuse me, would you mind stopping ..."

Beckett was not exactly forthcoming about his role in attracting investors to IIL. But the programme found out what happened from the victims who had been drawn into Ross's sting on the broker's advice. Isobel Hall, the programme reported, was persuaded that IIL was "such a good idea that unless she handed over her savings within seven days she would miss the boat."

Mrs Hall recalled the day she unwittingly said goodbye to her savings:

"I had a policy with Liberty Life and I had occasion to go to the Liberty Life offices to see about the policy which I had with them. While I was there, one of the managers approached me and asked if I had any other money to invest. I said yes, so inside about three to four days, a Mr Drew Beckett and one of his employees came to my house.

"I said I knew nothing about International Investments so he introduced it to me, and I told them that was all the money I had in the world as I was a widow and that was my security, and they said no problem, that it was a very sound investment."

Harry Duffin told "4 What It's Worth" a similar tale of woe.

"It was Drew Beckett who approached me. I did not approach anyone else. I was quite happy with the money where it was invested, but he said that he could get me 14 percent. I had then signed over the money to him.

"Someone stole my money, and I want it back."

The documentary's reporter added one observation which I would suggest really sums up the attitude the money-men have for their clients.

"When Isobel Hall and Harry Duffin were advised by Drew Beckett to invest their money with International Investments, the financial services act was not in force. However, Drew Beckett's company, Liberty Life Assurance, have since become a member of LAUTRO, one of the new organisations set up to protect investors. So Mr Beckett now has the official seal of approval to advise people on where best to invest their money."

In November 1983, Albert Braithwaite from Armagh contacted

Sovereign Financial Service for advice. The reply left him in no doubt; his money would be safe with International Investments. He still has the letter they sent him on November 18, 1983:

We suggest that this £5,000 should be invested in a Gibraltar based company called International Investments. This company (a licensed Merchant Bank) uses Gibraltar only to clear their funds, which are then invested into a worldwide portfolio. The Company guarantees a return of 13 percent tax free for the next two years. This means that the £5,000 will become £6,384.50 in two years.

Their funds are cleared and guaranteed by Barclays Bank International.

(This was an out-and-out lie on the part of IIL; Barclays Bank never supplied any such clearance or guarantee. But Albert wasn't to know that.)

Irresistible, wasn't it? I'm no mathematician, but even I can calculate that's a 27 percent profit in just two years. Tax free. If I hadn't been turned into a deeply cynical man by years in the private investigation business, it's the sort of offer I'd give some thought to myself.

Ross knew he had to do something when the investors began complaining their interest cheques were overdue. And he knew damn well that it was the brokers he had to keep happy, not the real victims of his multi-million pound scam. He had to talk down the worries, and he used all his canny charm to do it.

In a way even I have a grudging respect for the roguish way Finbarr Ross pulled off yet another coup. Even as his bank was collapsing around him, he still managed to drag in more money from the brokers. Ross decided the best way to allay the fears was to act, in the jargon of the financial world, in a 'bullish' fashion. If you show people you're a confident, go-ahead type, then like as not they'll follow you.

Early in October 1983 Ross sent out his circular to the Northern

Ireland brokers offering them the £500 bonus on top of any normal commission. He could then sit back and conjure up a picture of the drooling greed that letter would stir up. But he still had to give the brokers something to keep their clients' qualms at bay.

Ross threw a party, a lavish champagne shindig at the Stormont Hotel in Belfast. It was Christmas, 1983, and at that time of year no-one can resist a freebie, he reasoned, least of all a broker. He planned the party well, right down to the special gifts he gave out to staff nominated by the cartel.

Finbarr Ross, the well-heeled, sophisticated boss of International Investments, was in control. He chaired a brokers' meeting at the Stormont, and explained that any financial difficulties the company was experiencing were only temporary, a mere monetary blip on the path to fortune. IIL had assets, he revealed, mostly in property, worth millions. There was no need for alarm; just sit tight and it would be riches all round.

The brokers went away pledging new investments from their clients of around a million pounds.

It was the last time Finbarr Ross was ever seen again in Ireland, North or South.

• • •

Now please don't get me wrong. I'm not trying to say that there's no such thing as a decent, honest broker. In this case there were several. Or that any broker who advised investing in Ross's setup was inevitably unscrupulous. One broker, Gordon Hamill, acted in an honourable manner which went some small way, at least, to restoring my faith in the profession.

Mr Hamill had advised clients to put their money into International Investments just when it was about to go bankrupt. He did it completely innocently, and he made it a point of honour to see what he could do about getting that money back.

One client was repaid £2,600, from Mr Hamill's own pocket, because the broker felt so bad about giving unreliable investment advice. Mr Hamill has spent twice as much since then trying to get redress for the people who were duped.

But there's no denying that Ross had an uncanny power to charm some of the brokers. Here was a baby-faced rogue who could talk his way out of anything. The brokers, slavering for yet more cash, were like putty in his hands. But there was definitely a tragic irony played out at that party in the Stormont Hotel on December 15, 1983. Gifts and presents handed out, while all the time the clients' money was disappearing down International Investments' vast financial plughole.

Even when Ross fled Ireland for a life of luxury in the States the brokers still had an interesting role to play. I'm going to jump ahead a little in the story here, to 1984, by which time it was evident even to the brokers that all was far from well at IIL.

In January of that year a deputation of the brokers visited the company's office at 27, Leeson Park Dublin, the building shared by Ross's company and Frank Murray. Their mission was to confront Murray and Ronald Vincent to try to find out just what the hell was going on. It hardly needs saying that they were to leave unenlightened.

The next month, the same group took a trip to Houston, Texas, where Ross had set himself up in an apartment in the fashionable Chevy Chase area of the city.

Whatever means Ross used to charm the brokers at that gathering of grasping ambitions, he managed once more to escape with his personal coffers relatively unscathed. I've been able to establish that Ross told the deputation although there was the small matter of a £6.2 million shortfall at IIL, the American assets of the company were worth more than 10 million. How on earth Ross managed to persuade a group of financial experts that this bare-faced lie was fact is quite beyond me, but persuade them he did.

The brokers had gone to Ross to accuse him of gross mismanagement of their clients' funds, yet he ended the day better placed than before. The outcome of that meeting was quite extraordinary, and was to prove crucial in the next sordid stages of the International Investments story.

Ross struck a deal with the brokers. He suggested a simple pact to disarm them during heated argument. If they felt so strongly he was mismanaging International Investments, he said, why didn't they take over the company themselves? His only stipulation was that Ronald Vincent and Frank Murray remain in charge. Ross himself, naturally enough, would be paid a salary and become a director of IIL.

The brokers accepted, ignorant of the fact that all that remained in IIL's account in Gibraltar at that time was just £5,000 - not even enough to give its 1,200 investors a fiver each. George Finbarr Ross had pulled another masterstroke; the hapless middlemen were now at the helm of the sinking ship.

One of those brokers was Bryan Fryer-Kelsey, an investment advisor running his own Belfast-based company, Hampton Insurance and Investment Services. Once again, incidentally, Mr Kelsey's firm is now a member of FIMBRA, the United Kingdom regulatory body which gives the seal of respectability to investment advisors.

Bryan Fryer-Kelsey was another star of the "4 What It's Worth" documentary on International Investments. Reporter Susan Osman asked him: **"Are you going to reimburse those creditors that you encouraged to invest with International Investments?"**

His reply was brief. **"It is a silly question",** he told her. Ms Osman managed to fire off another couple of questions. Why did Mr Fryer-Kelsey and the Management Committee take control of the bank when Finbarr Ross fled to America? Did he feel any of the responsibility for the loss of £7 million that people invested, trusting his professional judgement? Mr Bryan Fryer-Kelsey drove off, leaving the questions unanswered.

So, our happy band of brokers returned from Texas with effective control of the ailing IIL. They met with Vincent and Murray to work out ways to defuse the growing pressure from their investors. They realised it would be well nigh impossible to get new investments from Northern Ireland - word was getting around about unpaid cheques and the suspicious affairs of the company. So they decided to solicit new investments elsewhere to pay the existing interest owed by IIL.

Ronald Vincent had one last attempt to get everyone off the hook. On March 22, 1984, he sent the worried investors a letter.

Remember David Mairs, the retired architect from County Antrim, whose family put £200,000 of their hard-earned savings into the avaricious hands of Finbarr Ross? At the beginning of April, 1984, the postman delivered him his copy of the IIL Managing Director's letter. It was Mr Mairs' first real inkling that things had gone drastically wrong.

You will be aware from Press, Radio and Television that national and world economy have started to recover from one of the longest periods of recession in history. Public and private companies operating in the U.K. and Ireland have been particularly vulnerable in the climate of strict U.K. monetarist policies.

International Investments Limited have further suffered from the exposure of a preponderance of southern Ireland's property in its portfolio as capital appreciation has failed to meet interest rates resulting in a severe liquidity problem. The demise of several financial institutions in recent years has inevitably led a large number of investors to request withdrawals at, and ahead of maturity.

International Investments Limited are not at this present time in a position to meet these requirements and we are confident that you will appreciate that a forced sale of assets in a depressed market would not

be in the interests of our depositors and could if pursued lead to a disastrous situation. However, the directors with the assistance of a management advisory committee feel that a breathing period and your cooperation will resolve the situation. The freezing of accrued and compound interest effective 31st December 1983 is a pre-requisite to a recovery. In this event it is proposed to invite all depositors to convert to shareholders' stock, this will have the immediate effect of securing our assets which are valued in the region of £4 million - £4,000,000.

A number of avenues could then be explored for an orderly disposal of assets which would secure the greater part, if not all, of your capital. You will be encouraged in the knowledge that to date depositors in excess of 1 million value have signified their agreement to this proposal. Please sign the attached form and return to your intermediary or direct to International Investments in the s.a.e. provided. Receipt will be acknowledged. Please act now as any delay is likely to prejudice success and could be expensive.

Slowly it dawned on David Mairs and the other investors what they were being asked to do. The letter from Vincent and his group of brokers was encouraging them to convert their deposits into shares. Rather than having money in a bank, they would actually own the bank. Imagine getting such a proposal from your normal High Street bank. It was obvious something was very wrong indeed.

Despite the emphasis in the letter that International Investments had £4 million worth of assets, the bank was not worth a single penny. It was the beginning of the end for investors' dreams. The coffers were empty.

Gordon Hamill, the Lurgan broker who has tried his best to get justice for his depositors, was astonished by his copy of the letter.

"I knew it was wrong. The brokers had no right to do it. They had

no power, and converting deposits to shares means that in the event of bankruptcy you have less rights to money back. They said they were doing it to save the company, but I asked for my money back. I was told I could not have it because it was in a suspense account. I found out later this was not true. The money was in an ordinary account in the Ulster Bank, but I could not get it then and by the time I found out it had gone."

Jim Noakes, the Isle of Man's Banking Commissioner who ran IIL off the island in 1983, summed up the feelings of many of those investors when he spoke to Channel 4's reporters:

"I do not think I can comment on that circular as a banking supervisor but, as a person, if a relative of mine received a circular like that, I would advise them to have nothing to do with it and to consult a lawyer immediately."

That's just what Emily Mairs decided to do. Other investors followed suit. And some of them consulted me.

• • •

Twelve hundred people were conned by George Finbarr Ross. By the end of April 1984, IIL had received £12.3 million from investors. About £1.4 million was from the savings of Irish men and women working in England - the money they hoped would one day bring them back home. In Northern Ireland the brokers brought Ross £5.5 million from investors, most of them pensioners looking for a safe place to put their life savings. Ross was no respecter of the cloth, either, one Protestant cleric and 15 Catholic priests were lured into his sting.

Such was the man's lust for wealth and status that he even sank to the degenerate depths of ripping off an old school friend. Joe Coughlan from Skibbereen, County Cork, had been a playground pal of George Finbarr Ross, and was later, coincidentally, to work alongside him at the Norwich Union. Obviously Joe trusted the guy. He handed over his life savings to Ross's Irish Investment Society, and Ross repaid that faith by transferring the cash to IIL without Joe's consent.

Joe Coughlan later swore on affidavit that **"George Finbarr Ross or some third party forged my name to effect such a transfer."**

When the whole affair blew up, Joe - whose mother had also trusted Ross with her savings - contacted his old pal in Houston. Ross **"led me to believe that he had considerable personal assets and that when the dust had settled on the affairs of International Investments Limited, he would pay me personally"**. Needless to say, he didn't.

Today those investors have little hope of ever seeing a penny of that money again. They are now only left with shattered dreams and ruined lives.

Harry Duffin: "It is gone. If you ever feel like crying that is the time to do it. All those years, all that hard work ... some person stole my money and I want it back.

"This man Ross is in America, and he is living off my money. I do not care how I get it back, but I will get it back one way or the other. I am not threatening anybody, I will do it lawfully, but I will get my money."

Isobel Hall: "It was just terrible . I was really devastated . In fact, I thought I was going to have a heart attack at the time. It was just terrible. To think that everything my husband had left me was just gone down the drain."

David Mairs: "When you have saved for your retirement, worked

out a safe and reasonably comfortable future without worries, it is absolutely dreadful to have it all taken away, especially by someone you have known and put your trust in."

If there was one letter among the thousands in my file on this whole iniquitous affair that really brought home what happened to the investors, it is this. Michael Spellman, whose wife invested in IIL, wrote encouraging me to keep the case going.

Dear Mr. Flynn - My wife Nora is in a home and has to be looked after. Her mind is gone. It is all over International Investments Ltd that has got her in such a fix. I am going to find out what can be done about the missing money. There is a suitcase of paper here about the matter.

I am Nora Spellman's husband and she does not have a clue what day of the week it is. She is in a bad way. So I say good luck.

The handwriting on the letter is that of a man under severe stress. And who is to blame for that? Remember Harry Duffin's words:

"I blame Finbarr Ross, but I blame the brokers even more. They are the ones who only live for their commission."

I often wonder whether George Finbarr Ross and the others who helped him escape justice feel the slightest twinge of remorse for the people who suffered in this shabby trickery. For people like David Mairs, confined to a wheelchair, with his retirement dreams in tatters.

Unlike Ross, David Mairs never got a second chance. He had no way of finding further funds to make the last years of his life tolerably comfortable. Isobel Hall will never recoup the money her husband saved for her. Nora Spellman's reward for her faith in International Investments is a life of bleakest tragedy.

Perhaps a miracle will happen. Maybe George Finbarr Ross, soaking up the Texan sun as he reads these words - I reckon it won't take long for his cronies to rush him a copy - will finally feel guilty. Perhaps he'll decide that it's not too late, that he can still try and pay back the money he stole?

On second thoughts, forget it. I'm a bit too old now to believe in Santa Claus.

Chapter Four

COMBING THE WRECKAGE

What kind of man would take on the job of sorting out the financial jumble that was International Investments? Back in May 1984, I would have said either a brave man or a fool.

Finbarr Ross had covered his tracks skillfully. The cunning cheat had been well aware that the more spurious companies and bank accounts he filtered the investors' money into the less likely it was to be traced. The result was a fiscal labyrinth that would have tried the patience of a dozen saints.

Ross had employed the trick used by swindlers since time began; hide the evidence in a maze so complex that eventually your pursuers are forced to admit defeat, rather than spend the rest of their days searching for a hundred needles in a thousand haystacks. Cover your tracks, in other words, with confusion.

By March 1984, Ronald Vincent was experiencing more than a little difficulty in deciding which way to turn. In agreeing with Frank Murray and the brokers to take over effective control of International Investments during that reassuring meeting with Ross in Texas, he had landed himself well and truly up to his neck in it. With debts running into millions, and just £5,000 in the accounts, IIL's Managing Director had been left holding a particularly demanding baby.

At the beginning of April the Gibraltar authorities finally took some action - better late than never, I suppose - and demanded up-to-date audited accounts of International Investments Ltd., ordering that a local firm of chartered accountants be appointed to do the job.

Ronald Vincent had already taken a good look at the company's 'accounts', such as they were, and was horrified by what he had found. He asked chartered accountant Timothy Revill, a former Isle of Man acquaintance with an office on Gibraltar's Main Street, to go over the books. Revill agreed, and the paper evidence of the company's hopeless insolvency was sent to Gibraltar from Leeson Park.

I said at the start of this chapter that only a brave man or a fool would have taken on the financial wreckage of IIL; I can only tell you Timothy Revill is no fool.

"Having seen the state of the books, Vincent realised he was a 'stooge director'", Revill recalls. After spending four days examining IIL's accounts - which were, to use his terse description, "in a hell of a mess" - the no-nonsense accountant said there was only one thing for it. Liquidation.

On June 12, 1984, IIL's shareholders agreed the company should be wound up. A week later, the Supreme Court of Gibraltar appointed Timothy Revill provisional liquidator.

The task ahead of him was immense. Creditors were owed a staggering £7.3 million sterling, and the company only had a few thousand pounds' worth of assets in its own name. But the level headed, methodical Revill refused to let such details intimidate him. Right from the beginning, he was in control; what's more, he felt full recovery was possible.

After Revill's appointment as liquidator was ratified at the end of July, he was given wide-ranging powers to investigate the company's affairs and to attempt to trace and recover its assets. This he proceeded to do with a speed and efficiency which more than justified his appointment. Finbarr Ross was up against a powerful adversary. For the people who had entrusted their life savings to IIL, it seemed there might after all be a chink of light at the end of the crooked Corkman's murky financial tunnel.

Let me make one thing quite clear. There is no doubt whatsoever in my mind that if Timothy Revill had been permitted to follow his liquidation through to the end, the vast majority of IIL's investors would have got most, possibly all, of their money back. George Finbarr Ross, might even have served a spell inside for the massive fraud he committed, would by now have sunk into the penniless obscurity every con-man deserves.

On a personal level: If, during the summer of 1984, Revill had been left to his own devices and been allowed to sort out the mess, the last eight years of my own life would have followed an entirely different path. Billy Flynn would today be a financially secure man. There would have been no need to put myself through the bankruptcies, the exhaustion, the endless alternation of triumphs and disappointments that since 1984 my professional life has become.

And there would have been no need for this book.

• • •

Timothy Revill was the perfect choice for the International Investments salvage job. A chartered accountant with 10 years experience, a partner in the respected Gibraltar firm of Smith, Forshaw, Harper and Revill, when it came to the lengths to which people will go to make a fast buck there wasn't a lot he hadn't seen.

Revill was capable of mixing it with the best and the worst of them, of taking on board the wheeling and dealing central to the world of high finance; yet he had managed to retain his own code of ethics, linked to a strong sense of responsibility and fair play, that would have been incomprehensible to Finbarr Ross.

An honest man who understood the minds of dishonest men. That was Timothy Revill then, and that is Timothy Revill now. IIL's investors couldn't have wished for a better liquidator, but his very efficiency in tracking down their misappropriated money was to prove his downfall.

Like I said, Revill was initially appointed provisional liquidator of the company, with limited powers to collect up its assets and begin writing up its books. This he lost no time in doing, and soon one fact became glaringly obvious to his trained accountant's eye. Finbarr Ross and Frank Murray had, almost from IIL's inception, gradually bled the company dry for their own gain.

In the report he was to send to creditors, Revill summed up an audacious fraud in these telling lines.

I am .. of the opinion that misfeasance and misappropriation has occurred on a large scale by a number of those involved in the management and administration of the company and that the illegal aspects of this require scrutiny by the authorities.

Revill realised that if he was to make any headway at all in the liquidation, he'd need the authority to take proceedings in Ireland and the USA to recover assets rightfully owned by IIL. There was also the matter of £1.5 million worth of debts in Ireland owing to the company, which, being secured by property, Revill believed were fully recoverable. On the advice of his Gibraltar lawyer Peter Caruana, he successfully applied to the Supreme Court of Gibraltar for more official muscle. In the words of his report to creditors:

On the 3rd July 1984 the Court granted me wider powers, in particular to employ legal advisors, and to begin legal action in other jurisdictions to recover assets and to employ (Ronald) Vincent for a period of two months only, to assist me in tracing and recovering the assets of the company, about which I had scant details at that date.

Revill's employment of IIL's "stooge director" was to rebound on him later - but as he said recently: "Obviously, you employ the people who have been working within the company to unravel a hell of a mess. (Vincent) was a very willing co-operator - he behaved in quite a proper manner. He assisted me greatly in leading me to the assets of the company." Vincent was employed at a salary of £1,500 per month. Although they had been nodding acquaintances on the Isle of Man, the two men had no business dealings prior to the IIL liquidation.

Revill then contacted Houston law firm Fulbright and Jaworski, and retained attorney Samuel Stubbs to supervise the American end of the liquidation. This was vital; he believed Finbarr Ross had filtered at least £5 million of the investors' missing money into personal concerns in Houston and Dallas. Stubbs was instructed to issue immediate proceedings against Ross in an attempt to recover the cash, and employed a private detective, Ed Panku, to assist in uncovering Ross's maze of hidden American assets and bank accounts. Fulbright and Jaworski were paid $25,000 on account, with an assurance that there was a further $75,000 on call to pay subsequent fees.

On July 16, Timothy Revill travelled to Dublin and went about the business of, in his words, "freezing whatever assets I came across." These included paintings, racehorses, and properties. He paid solicitors Arthur Cox and Co. a deposit of £5,000 to act for him in Ireland, and chartered accountant Vincent O'Neill £3,000 to take on the role of his Dublin agent.

I obtained an interim injunction in the High Court in Dublin (wrote Revill in his report) **restraining Ross and other associated persons from dealing in or disposing of assets in Ireland controlled by them, but which I maintained were paid for with funds from International.**

On July 20, under the headline **£6.25m BANK COLLAPSE ASSETS MUST BE HELD**, the Irish Times reported:

Some £6.25m. is unaccounted for in a Gibraltar investment company which has several Irish associations, it was claimed in the High Court in Dublin yesterday.

The claim was made to Mr. Justice Keane by the provisional liquidator of International Investments Ltd., which is registered in Gibraltar and until recently held a banking licence there.

The liquidator, Mr. Timothy J. Revill, was granted an interim

injunction against nine named defendants, most of them with addresses in Ireland. Under a separate interim injunction, George Finbarr Ross, stated to be an Irish citizen, and whose address was given as c/o Shawnee Operations Co., Houston, Texas, was restrained from selling or disposing of certain assets within the jurisdiction so as to reduce their value below £5 million sterling.

The newspaper then printed a list of the assets Ross was prevented from selling, which included 90 shares in Anchor Properties, registered in the name of solicitor Paul Smithwick; 10 shares in Anchor Properties in the name of Frank Murray; and shares in Shelmar (Investments), Shelmar (Holdings) and Centenary Investments, registered in the names of solicitors Ailbhe Rice and Paul Smithwick.

The list of interim injunctions granted against defendants in Ireland included the names of Paul Smithwick, Frank Murray and Ailbhe Rice. An interim injunction was also granted against Finbarr Ross's second wife Sheila Canty, who was living at the £500,000 solar house in Clonee her husband had built with IIL funds, preventing her from selling or disposing of the house or its contents.

It was stated (the Irish Times report concluded) that on June 19th, Mr. Revill was appointed provisional liquidator. Since that date, he has been trying to get information relating to the company's assets. He found himself in a situation where there was considerable Irish association between the persons who managed the company and those who held themselves out as directors ... The interim injunctions were effective until Monday week.

Revill was making progress fast.

On July 27, the Supreme Court of Gibraltar heard the petition to wind up the company, which had been brought forward from October because of urgent public concern. The court ordered that IIL be wound up; that Revill should be appointed liquidator (thus ratifying his provisional appointment); and that Revill should be deemed to have all the duties of the Official Receiver.

In a letter dated August 3, Timothy Revill wrote to IIL's investors:

I can now inform you that an Order for Winding Up of the above company was made by the Supreme Court in Gibraltar on Friday 27 July and by a subsequent Order I was appointed Liquidator ...

The legal action I took in Ireland .. has, I am pleased to say, resulted in the handing over to me of all the identified assets there by those in whose names they were registered. The action in the U.S.A. is at an advanced stage of preparation.

Throughout this period a team of my staff have been piecing together information ... Due to the virtual total lack of books of account, I am afraid that this exercise is going to take some time yet, since our starting point is 1976.

You will see from the enclosed note that the meeting of creditors is to be held in Gibraltar ... It may be that you will not wish or be able to travel to Gibraltar for the meeting, in which case I would suggest that you appoint a proxy to represent you ... If you wish to be represented you should send your proxy form .. to either one of the Barristers or myself, or anybody else who will be attending the meeting.

An enclosed note informed creditors that the meeting would be held three weeks hence, on August 24.

In the interim, Timothy Revill wasted no time. He applied for and was given the power to start further legal proceedings in the United States and elsewhere. Thanks to the work of Houston private detective Ed Panku in addition to his own investigations, Revill knew that the bulk of the investors' money had been salted away by Finbarr Ross into a maze of bank accounts, properties and oil wells deep in the heart of Texas.

On August 7, he boarded a plane for Houston. He was going to get that money back.

• • •

Now you may be asking yourself - where was all the cash coming from to pay for this liquidation? I've already mentioned the $25,000 paid on deposit to Fulbright and Jaworski, with a further $75,000 on call - if there's such a thing as a cheap American law firm, I've yet to hear about it - plus private detective Ed Panku's fees. Then there was the £5,000 to Dublin solicitors Arthur Cox, £3,000 to Dublin chartered accountant Vincent O'Neill, Ronald Vincent's £1,500 per month salary - and that's before you even start thinking about remuneration for Revill himself. Conducting a liquidation costs money, and IIL didn't have any - not in its own name, anyway. So who was supplying the funds?

At the start of the liquidation, Timothy Revill's lawyer in Gibraltar, Peter Caruana, asked his client that very same question. The methodical Revill had explained to Caruana the need to retain legal advisors in Ireland and the USA if the missing millions were to be recovered. But legal advisors, his lawyer pointed out, cost money. Where's the money coming from?

Not from 186 Main Street, Gibraltar, that's for sure. A thorough examination of IIL's office there had turned up the princely sum of two pence. But among the files, Revill had discovered that the company held an account at Williams & Glynn's Bank on the Isle of Man. And that account held £9,000.

It was a start. That £9,000 covered the initial payments to Arthur Cox and Vincent O'Neill. As for the $25,000 paid to the Houston law firm, Revill had managed to obtain this sum, plus the guarantee of a further $75,000, from the Government of Gibraltar. How he went about this gives us a fair idea of the extent to which authorities on the Rock considered themselves negligent over the whole IIL fiasco.

If Timothy Revill and I share one thing in common, it's our stubborn streak. We don't give up easily. When Revill originally approached the Government for cash to fund the liquidation, he was turned down. But following several meetings with Gibraltar's banking supervisor, C.C. Bruton, his superiors decided that it might be a good idea to grant Revill's request after all.

To achieve this, the chartered accountant used a powerful combination of hard facts and psychology. He brought home to Bruton the negligence displayed by his department in failing to monitor IIL's affairs in Gibraltar. He reminded Bruton that a banking licence is not in itself an authority to conduct such business; under the UK Banking Act, to do this a company has to obtain permission from the authorities. IIL hadn't asked for, nor been given, any such permission - making its entire operation in Gibraltar illegal from start to finish.

Revill went on to speculate on the possible repercussions, and suggested it might be more economical for Gibraltar to fund the American proceedings than be the defendants in a multi-million pound action brought about by investors against the Gibraltar authorities, as had happened after the Barnett Christie collapse in Guernsey.

His remarks were relayed by Burton to Gibraltar's Financial and Development Secretary, Brian Traynor, and Attorney-General Eric Thistlethwaite. The $25,000 duly appeared, plus the promise of another $75,000 in reserve. But Revill's tough tactics hadn't endeared him to the Rock's authorities.

They had good reason to feel uneasy about what this ruthlessly efficient accountant was unearthing. What action would Revill take if he discovered that not only had IIL broken the terms of its Gibraltar banking licence 27 times and got away with it, but that from 1983 to 1984, when Finbarr Ross and Frank Murray were still soliciting investments, IIL was operating with no banking licence at all yet still using its Gibraltar address? For the last year of its existence, IIL's operation on the Rock had been wholly illegal - and totally unchecked.

As for Ronald Vincent's £1,500 per month salary, this was being met by Revill's firm, Smith, Forshaw Harper & Revill, until such time as there was cash in the liquidator's account. Revill himself worked for nothing, confident that once the liquidation was complete he would be paid out of the assets he was already beginning to recover.

And despite certain insidious claims made later to the contrary, that was how the only truly effective period of International Investments' liquidation - the two-month period under Timothy Revill immediately after the company's collapse - was financed.

• • •

On August 7 1984, Revill arrived in Houston, Texas, with his solicitor Peter Caruana. The purpose of the trip was to freeze all American assets in Finbarr Ross's name, and the ground had already been prepared for him; Samuel Stubbs had filed a federal lawsuit against Ross and drawn up an application for a temporary restraining order and a temporary injunction preventing him from disposing of any assets directly or indirectly belonging to IIL.

Stubbs' impression of Revill was favourable: "(He) prepared his facts and figures. He was extremely good, a professional accountant, on top of things", he was to say later.

A detailed account of the crucial next ten days in Houston can be found in Chapter 6. Suffice to say that on Saturday, August 18, Revill and Caruana arrived back in Gibraltar euphoric and triumphant after an exhausting week in and out of court. They had managed to obtain a Texas court order restraining Finbarr Ross from disposing of an estimated £5.2 million assets acquired with IIL's funds. Add to this the injunction obtained in Dublin on July 19, and it seemed that success was well within Revill's grasp. Both he and Caruana agreed that what had only two months before looked like a hopeless case - a company with just £5,000 in recognisable assets, and over £7 million in debts - was now far from it. The two men agreed they would convene a meeting of investors in Northern Ireland in October they were certain that, by then, they would have some good news to give them at last.

Only one thing was puzzling Peter Caruana. On the plane back from Houston, he had been reading the full transcript of Ross's deposition to the court. Why, he wondered, had Ross's counsel requested that his clients' banking details not be made available until after August 24? But Caruana put it out of his mind. Victory, after all, was theirs. Why spoil the taste of it by worrying about technicalities?

Timothy Revill was now fully confident that if all the assets disclosed in Texan were realised, and various legal actions were taken against third parties, full recovery was a real possibility. In other words, on August 18 1984, it looked as if the 1,200 investors ripped off by Finbarr Ross and his bogus bank would be getting their money back.

And as I said earlier, I am in no doubt that if Timothy Revill had been allowed to continue with the liquidation, they would have done.

•••

Back in Gibraltar, Revill was putting the finishing touches to his report to the creditors. A professional, detailed analysis of the fraudulent free-for-all that went by the name of International Investments Ltd., it said all that needed to be said.

The report's message was as clear as day: IIL was a swindle from beginning to end.

Having given a brief history of the establishment of the company, Revill detailed the conditions under which Finbarr Ross managed to obtain a Gibraltar banking licence. In the light of what we now know to have happened to the investors' money, those conditions make interesting reading:

(i) Not less than 90% of the sum of deposits received should be deposited in a bank in Gibraltar approved by the Financial and Development Secretary.

(ii) Any deposits received by the company that were not deposited by it in Gibraltar should be deposited in a registered bank in Jersey.

(iii) The deposits in Gibraltar or Jersey were not to be used for any purpose other than:

(a) Repayments to depositors.

(b) Payment, if required, in respect of any financial guarantee given by the Company in return for which adequate security has been received by the Company.

(c) Loans to the residents of the Republic of Ireland, provided that no loans should be made that would have the effect of making the aggregate loans outstanding, at the close of business on the day of making the loans, to more than 90% of the amount due to depositors at the close of business on the previous day. ,

(d) Investment.

Just a brief glance at the conditions of the licence proves that Finbarr

Ross was breaking virtually every banking rule in Gibraltar's book while the authorities were just sitting back and letting it happen. As James Galliano, a Gibraltarian accountant whose name will soon become as familiar to you as Revill's, told a reporter recently: "(Ross) got a blank cheque in Gibraltar to operate with no supervision. It couldn't happen now." I would sincerely hope not.

Later on in Revill's report, he examines the fraudulent manner in which International Investments dealt with investors' money:

International did not operate as a bank insofar as it did not keep a matched maturity book of deposits and assets, but instead invested a large proportion of its deposits in various property holdings and developments in Ireland and the U.S.A. For a number of reasons, interest arising within the company did not match interest payable to depositors, and deposit interest was in fact being paid out of new capital that was being raised. Even up until February of 1984, deposits were still being raised and employed in paying December 1983 interest payments .. although at that stage Ross and Murray knew full well that the company was in financial difficulties.

Robbing Peter, in other words, to pay Paul. Or robbing John, Frank, Jim and David to pay Finbarr ...

The books of account of the company (continued the report) consisted principally of numerous cash receipts and cash payments books. It appears that these cash books were not summarised nor reconciled to bank statements. The analysis of payments and receipts is incomplete and in most cases inaccurate ... the appalling state of the cash books has in fact necessitated their re-writing from Day 1, by my staff.

Other eccentric accounting methods used by IIL and revealed in

Revill's report included cheques being used on a random basis instead of in numbered sequence, and no general ledger being kept. Finbarr Ross had been pulling the old trick of covering his tracks with confusion. Unfortunately (for him), Ross hadn't bargained for an opponent with the patience and tenacity of Timothy Revill.

Then there were the loans. Considering it was run by a man for whom the personal accumulation of cash meant so much, IIL seemed surprisingly relaxed and generous with the people to whom it lent money.

With regard to the making of loans by International (wrote Revill) it appears that there was little or no system of checking the credit rating of the borrower, and no proper documentation was made to record these loans. In the majority of cases no security was taken. Loans were made to both third parties and to subsidiaries of International, and I have found virtually no repayment of either capital or interest on outstanding balances over the last two years ...

Many of these loans are currently the subject of litigation through Mr. Oliver Conlon, a solicitor who was heavily involved in many of the property transactions financed by International and who himself received personal loans from International.

And, later in the report:

The ultimate destination of a large part of International's funds is not yet apparent since they were channelled through Ross's personal accounts in the U.K. and the United States. Also a very considerable flow of funds through the client's solicitor, Oliver Conlon .. has yet to be accounted for.

Altogether, it was a damning report - but one which must have reassured many of the individuals who had been ripped off by Finbarr Ross. For one thing the report made clear was that Revill understood the workings of IIL inside out. Already, he had coolly and efficiently managed to trace and freeze the majority of Ross's illgotten assets. With a man as proficient as that in charge of the liquidation, it was surely only a matter of time before the investors would be getting their missing money back.

Timothy Revill's report was presented to the first creditors' meeting, at the Catholic Community Centre in Gibraltar, on August 24, 1984.

On the same day, Revill was removed as liquidator of International Investments Ltd. His successor was a mild-mannered Gibraltarian accountant named James Galliano. It's fair to speculate that if Mr. Galliano had known what he was getting himself into, he would never have taken over the liquidation.

•••

From Timothy Revill to IIL investors, 20 September 1984:

As you know, the First Meeting of the Creditors of "International" was held in Gibraltar on Friday 24th August, and I am now writing to you to give you a summary of the proceedings of the meeting ...

The Creditors' Meeting was attended by creditors and proxies totalling just over £4 million of which Mr Colm Allen, a Dublin Barrister, held proxies for £3.2 million.

As liquidator, I presented the meeting with a summary of the affairs of International leading up to the Petition for Winding Up, and a progress report of the subsequent liquidation to date.

Suggestions were made at the meeting, and I understand also in

Ireland, that because my firm occupied the position of auditors (as instructed by the Commissioner of Banking) during the two-month period immediately preceding the Petition, that therefore I do not truly represent the interest of creditors in the subsequent liquidation. Those suggesting this are therefore inevitably implying that I have not conducted the liquidation in the best interests of the creditors.

It has also been brought to my attention that certain persons are circulating in Ireland allegations that I have paid myself £4,000 per week out of the company's funds and have employed (Ronald) Vincent at the exorbitant salary of £1,500 p.w.

I wish to take the opportunity to state that none of these allegations have any basis in truth ... far from having received fees at the rate of £4,000 per week, I have, in fact, as yet received no fees whatsoever for my services as liquidator .. and have funded all disbursements out of my firm's resources.

Finally, Mr. Vincent was employed by me with the specific approval of the Supreme Court for a period of two months only on a salary of £1,500 per month (my italics - B.F.) ... to enable me rapidly to identify and secure assets of the company about which there were little or no records.

Based on the above, the following two Resolutions were passed: -

First Motion:

'"Resolved that it is the wish of the creditors of International Investments Limited that Mr James Patrick Galliano ... be nominated the Liquidator of the company in the place of the Official Receiver and

Mr Timothy J Revill and that the appropriate application be made to the Court.

Second Motion:

"Resolved that an application be made to the Court for the appointment of a Committee of Inspection to act with the Liquidator and that such cor ittee of Inspection should be composed of the followinq: -

Mr Colm Allen
Dr John Lowe
Mr Bryan Fryer-Kelsey
Mr John Barbour
Dr Marcus Gregory"

I am concerned that no person previously responsible for the company's management or investments, its failure, or the recruitment of deposits, should now be concerned with the conduct of the winding up. I am therefore bringing to the notice of the Court certain facts within my possession with regard to the proposed members of the Committee of Inspection.

You could be forgiven for thinking something strange was going on. And you may be asking - who are these five men who made up the "Committee of Inspection"?

Colm Allen was a Dublin barrister who would become the Chairman of the Committee. Through solicitor Barry Manning, Allen had represented Finbarr Ross's business partner Frank Murray in court.

Top left - Frank Kelly and Billy Flynn in Gibraltar to meet Harech Budhrani.

Top right - London depositors Pat Murray, a native of Keady County Armagh is comforted by Patrick Kearney a native of County Donegal, both lost £70,000 their entire life savings.

Bottom - David Mairs - The Mairs family entrusted £200,000 to Finbarr Ross.

Top - I.I.L.'s Houston Headquarters which never existed.

Bottom Left - Mark Smith, a journalist with the Sunday Independent.

Bottom right - Coleman Cassidy, a journalist with the Sunday Press.

George Finbarr Ross.

Top - Declan Collins of Stokes, Kennedy & Crowley who intimidated the current Government Chief Whip on December the 8th 1990 to keep his nose out of the affair.

Bottom - Noel Dempsey T.D. for Meath

Roy Beggs, M.P. for East Antrim.

Top - Charles Haughey amongst friends.

Bottom - Brian Lenihan with Tanaiste John Wilson.

Top half page - Houston lawyer, Samuel Stubbs.

Bottom left - Alan Dukes.
Bottom right - Roger Garland.

Top - Geraldine Kennedy.

Bottom - Bobby Molloy. Current Minister in the Irish Government.

On July 30, 1984, less than four weeks before Revill's removal as liquidator, Manning had filed an affidavit to the High Court in Dublin on behalf of Murray, denying that Murray was chairman of International Investments and stating that he had no involvement in the management or administration of the company. Thanks to his counsel Colm Allen's sterling work, Murray walked from the court scot free.

(It was Frank Murray, you may remember, who shared Finbarr Ross's Leeson Park office and was in the habit of signing himself "Chairman" on IIL documents. According to Revill's report to creditors: **The signatories on (International Investments) accounts were generally Ross, together with, variously, Murray, Nuala Hussey, Patricia Kidney and G. McNamara, the latter three being administrative and secretarial assistants.)**

Bryan Fryer-Kelsey and John Barbour were brokers from Northern Ireland, some of whose clients had lost heavily as a result of their advice to invest in IIL. Dr. Marcus Gregory and Dr. John Lowe were creditors.

•••

From the Sunday Independent, October 13 1991:

The liquidator of the formerly Irish-controlled offshore company International Investments Ltd. (IIL), has announced he is to submit his resignation.

Gibraltar-based chartered accountant James Galliano has been unhappy for some time with his role in a liquidation in which he can make no further progress ...

Mr Galliano was appointed as liquidator of the company seven years ago, in circumstances which he now feels created expectations of him

that cannot be realised.

'I wish', he told me, 'I hadn't become involved.'

His predecessor as liquidator, Timothy Revill, still feels he should not have been replaced in a proxy vote in August 1984. 'I feel that the liquidation of IIL under me was conducted in a perfectly proper manner', he said. 'I still regret the circumstances which brought about my being replaced.'

Mr. Galliano will submit his resignation to a meeting of the company's creditors next month. This is his second attempt to stand down - his previous offer to relinquish the post, in 1987, was rejected by Gibraltar's Attorney-General.

In November '91, James Galliano finally succeeded in his long-held ambition to shake off the farcical nightmare that, for him, the liquidation had become. I wish him well; despite everything, despite being pushed from pillar to post for seven years, he remains the gentleman he was when we first met in 1984.

To succeed Galliano, I nominated London chartered accountant Tim Clunie and Gibraltar Finance Services Commission member John Bassett as joint liquidators. The brokers, meanwhile, nominated Gibraltar's Official Receiver in the hope that, after all this time, he might decide there was no point in continuing with the liquidation. At the time of writing (September '92) no-one knows what the hell's going on - which you could say sums up the IIL liquidation from the time Galliano took over.

Timothy Revill, who in 1984 was on the point of cracking the case for the creditors, has moved across the border into Spain where he now works at ECS Financial Management in Soto Grande. I'm glad to say his circumstances haven't changed - he is still a successful, respected chartered accountant. The IIL fiasco is well behind Revill, yet, even now, he admits to a desire to see fair play for the victims of Finbarr Ross's fraud.

"If I didn't need to earn a living and support a family", he says, "I'd like to get back on this case .. it's made me very disillusioned in the powers that be and their apparent lack of any genuine desire to see justice done. Seven million pounds of depositors' money ripped-off isn't something that just disappears."

•••

I have to admit that, at first, I too was taken in by the smears that in the summer of 1984 were being spread around regarding Revill's conduct in the liquidation. I had been led to believe that Revill was charging £20,000 a week for his services, and I knew nothing about his successful proceedings against Ross in Houston. I doubted, at worst, his integrity; at best, his efficiency.

The first time I spoke to Timothy Revill was on the phone on August 23, the eve of that fateful creditors' meeting. I had previously made at least a dozen attempts to speak to the man I wrongly believed was making a pig's ear of the liquidation.

When we finally connected, I told Revill in no uncertain terms what I thought. I told him he hadn't been performing his duties as liquidator in a fit and proper manner.

"To suggest that", Revill responded, "is lunacy."

I demanded a response from Revill concerning the allegations that he was charging £20,000 per week for the liquidation. "Only a madman would suggest that", he replied, adding that the situation was quite the opposite; his firm was over £20,000 out of pocket thanks to the IIL liquidation.

Revill concluded by saying that in his opinion there was no point in continuing the conversation, and I would receive a copy of his report in due course. He then put the phone down on me.

I have to say now that I don't blame him. I like to think I am blessed with pretty sound judgement when it comes to my fellow-man, but in the case of Timothy Revill it temporarily failed me. In my defence, I had never met him and knew nothing about the impressive progress he had made in just two months in tracing IIL's assets. I had heard the same claims about Revill's exorbitant fees that the investors had, and had no way of knowing those allegations were totally untrue - part of a widespread campaign to discredit the man who, more than anyone, was acting in the best interests of the investors.

"The thing that upset me at the time", Revill said recently, "was that I kept receiving letters that brought tears to my eyes from poor little depositors who had lost everything. At the same time, Ross was living very comfortably in Houston ... my legal perception of the whole IIL case is that it's all been done according to the law, but there's a big difference between going through the motions and what is actually being achieved."

I have had more than my fair share of depositor's letters over the years - boxes of them, in fact - and yet, even now, they never fail to move me. Each one contains the story of a human being ruined by a callous con-man, which is bad enough. But what has kept me on this case for eight years - what has provided the spur that has kept me going - is not the fraud perpetrated by George Finbarr Ross. He is, when you get down to it, no more than a cheap crook with a knack of charming cash out of people. There have been many like him, and I fear there will be many more.

No. What angers me is a system that is so cynical, so corrupt, so driven by greed, that it can not only allow people like Ross to get away with their crimes, but seemingly encourage them to do so. A system that, back in 1984, facilitated the removal from his duties of one of the few people involved in IIL's affairs after its collapse who genuinely wanted to see its investors get their money back. Timothy Revill didn't care two hoots about the brokers who had recommended Ross's financial Bermuda Triangle to their clients; his only concern was for the victims.

"At the risk of appearing naive to some, I am personally deeply disturbed at the general immorality that exists in this case", he would reflect eighteen months after the above events. Naive, no; decent, yes. Decency is a quality you don't come across often these days, and the day Revill was removed as liquidator of International Investments was also the day Finbarr Ross was demoted from his position as chief villain of the whole sorry saga.

On August 24, 1984, the system succeeded him.

Chapter Five

A BRIEFCASE FULL OF PROXIES

I am not a rich man. Few in my profession are. Even the fictitious Philip Marlowe hardly lived a life of luxury - the poor gent often didn't know where his next bottle of bourbon was coming from.

While there've been many occasions in the past eight years when I've wondered where to find the next mortgage payment, I never got a taste for bourbon. Brandy is more my drink, but only on my days off - unlike Marlowe, I don't usually indulge when I'm on a case. And unlike Marlowe, I wouldn't resort to violence. I'd rather fight with my wits than my fists.

But let's assume for a minute that I am both rich and violent. Let's imagine I have viciously battered someone to death, and while running from the scene of the crime, drenched in the victim's blood, have been caught with the murder weapon in my hand. All the evidence is against me. As far as the police are concerned, it's an open-and- shut case - it seems nothing can save me from a life sentence.

What would I do? I'd instruct my solicitor to retain the services of named Colm Allen. If anyone could help me, he could.

Colm Michael Allen, Barrister-at-Law, former Treasurer of the Bar Council, is thought to possess one of the smartest legal minds in Ireland. He knows the laws of the land inside out. If there's any weakness in a case, any loophole to be found, he will find it. And he is a brilliant orator; many verdicts have been swayed by the power of his polemic.

In court, Colm Allen shows no compassion towards witnesses who have the audacity to obstruct his client's case. He will, eloquently and mercilessly, tear their credibility to shreds. And he has a skill essential to any successful lawyer. He can let fly with the most outlandish rhetoric and make it sound reasonable.

A recent instance of this came at the Beef Tribunal, the Irish Government's lengthy enquiry into certain alleged practices at the Goodman beef processing plants. Allen was counsel for one of the players in the drama, Oliver Murphy, the former boss of the Hibernia Meats company. In the course of the tribunal it was revealed that Hibernia had donated £25,000 to Fianna Fail a few weeks before the party's triumph in the March 1987 election. In October that year the new FF government approved $46 million worth of insurance cover to Hibernia. The next month, Hibernia donated a further £25,000 to the party's funds.

Colm Allen's pronouncement to the Tribunal?

"Any slur or nasty, snide, whingeing, carping suggestion that there was anything involved in these contributions, other than the legitimate support of the legitimate democratic process, is beneath contempt."

A classic example of Allen in action. I would ask you to read that quote once again - it gives you more of an insight into the man's personality, both in and out of court, than ten thousand words from me ever could.

Colm Allen, a colleague once said, could convince a jury Hitler was a saint. As many of his grateful clients have found over the years, he is a useful man to have on your side.

And as Timothy Revill discovered back in 1984, he makes a ruthless and lethal adversary.

• • •

In mid-July 1984, it seemed the liquidation of IIL was going Timothy Revill and the investors' way. In the High Court in Dublin on the 19th, Revill had obtained an interim injunction preventing Finbarr Ross and his associates from disposing of the company's assets controlled by them in Ireland. On the 30th, in his absence, Revill obtained a further interim injunction, filed on his behalf by his Dublin solicitors Arthur Cox and Company. But, this time, not everything went smoothly.

Frank Murray, International Investments' Chairman, was in court to contest the proceedings against him. Murray, Finbarr Ross's right-hand man, was represented by solicitor Barry Manning of Edge, Manning & Co., and his barrister, junior counsel Colm Allen. Manning had filed an affidavit on Murray's behalf denying his client was IIL's Chairman - denying, in fact, that he had anything to do with the running of the company.

Perhaps, in fairness to Colm Allen, he may not have been aware of the existence of IIL documents and company cheques bearing Frank Murray's signature, with the title 'Chairman' inscribed in Murray's handwriting on several of the documents. Colm Allen informed Justice Keane that his client took "great offence" at being joined in these proceedings, and sought an order for them to be dismissed.

Sitting at the back of the court was a man who two months before had never heard of Frank Murray, Finbarr Ross or International Investments. His knowledge of Ross's audacious swindle was still sketchy, but he was learning fast. Since this man had taken a phone call from a distraught investor in May and agreed to investigate what had happened to his missing £7,000, he had already begun to learn far more than he ever wanted to about the fraudulent world of offshore finance. Now this observer was witnessing a man he knew to be a crook just about to get off scot free - and nobody was lifting a finger to stop it happening.

You've guessed it. The observer at the back of the court was one Billy Flynn.

I watched the proceedings that warm July day with increasing frustration. Frank Murray's counsel was defending him on grounds I knew to be completely false. What's more, Timothy Revill's legal representatives were offering no opposition to Colm Allen's application for proceedings against Murray to be dismissed.

Believe me, I was far from new to the things done in the name of justice, but what was happening in the High Court that day shocked me. Even now it never ceases to amaze me how wrong can miraculously become right in a court of law.

I had to do something. Mr. Justice Keane had already begun to give his decision on Colm Allen's application. Frank Murray, the man I knew was up to his neck in a massive fraud that had left hundreds penniless, was about to leave the High Court a free man.

Standing up, I interrupted the judge in mid-flow. I told him in no uncertain terms that while I was not a party to the proceedings, I told the court I was in possession of certain information that would suggest Frank Murray's affidavit was untrue, and therefore statements made on his behalf by Colm Allen were also untrue. Allen responded that my allegations were groundless, and I should be held in contempt of court.

Mr. Justice Keane advised me that since I wasn't a named party in the proceedings, he couldn't allow my allegations; I suggested he might consider an adjournment while I briefed Revill's lawyers on certain issues. Colm Allen's response was to apply for me to be committed.

The judge turned down this request but granted Allen his application; Timothy Revill's proceedings against Frank Murray were dismissed. Murray walked from the High Court without a stain on his character.

That was the first time I saw Colm Allen in action, and I hoped it would be the last. I had no way of knowing then just how central to the IIL affair he would become.

• • •

'Proxy' is one of those words which, said more than five times in a row, begins to sound ridiculous. But if you hold the majority of proxies on behalf of a company's shareholders, the result is far from foolish. You have in your possession a powerful voting weapon, to be used to change company policy at an annual general meeting, for instance.

Or, if the company's in liquidation, at a creditors' meeting.

It was the afternoon of Thursday August 23, three weeks after Frank Murray's triumph in Dublin's High Court, and the eve of the first meeting of IIL's investors. Timothy Revill was sitting in his Gibraltar office putting the finishing touches to his liquidator's report. He was rightly proud of it - as a comprehensive financial history of the farrago that was International Investments, it has yet to be bettered.

At 4.55 pm, five minutes before the final deadline for filing proxies, Revill's secretary Marguerite buzzed through to his office and told him two Irish gentlemen were in reception and wanted to see him urgently. Their names, she said, were Colm Allen and Barry Manning.

Revill had heard of neither of the men, but told Marguerite to show them in. At that moment, his attention was distracted by a phone call from another individual whose name meant nothing to him at the time - a private investigator from Ireland called Billy Flynn. Details of our conversation, which I now wish had never happened, can be found towards the end of Chapter 4.

Having, with good reason, put the phone down on me, Revill turned to apologise to Allen and Manning for keeping them waiting. With hardly a word, they slapped 410 proxies down on his desk and walked out of the office.

Now, as I've said, Timothy Revill maintains a strong sense of responsibility and fair play in all he does; an old-fashioned, professional attitude that is incomprehensible to some modern businessmen. Revill had never heard of Colm Allen or Barry Manning, was unfamiliar with this new pushy manner of doing business which was to typify the 1980s, and simply assumed the two brusque Irishmen were in a hurry. He didn't suspect for a moment that the 410 proxies on his desk spelt the end of his brief period as IIL's liquidator. And they'd been delivered with just minutes to spare.

Equally, Timothy Revill had no idea that a week earlier on August 17, the day he obtained the court order against Ross in Houston, Colm Allen had faxed a report from Gibraltar to Frank Murray and investment broker Bryan Fryer-Kelsey in Dublin. Allen's report, which contained defamatory allegations about the way Revill had been conducting the liquidation, was passed on by Murray and Fryer-Kelsey to a group of five brokers in the North.

If you remember, it was the eagerness of many of the brokers to believe Finbarr Ross's assurances of financial stability, the enthusiasm with which they persuaded their clients to sink their savings into the Cork con-man's spurious company, and the alacrity with which they (the brokers) accepted thank-you 'gifts' from Ross in return, that led to 1,200 investors losing a total of £7 million.

My investigations disclosed that the five brokers who were sent Allen's report by Murray and Fryer-Kelsey had taken over beneficial ownership of IIL just prior to its collapse in June. This fact was kept from Timothy Revill during his entire period as the company's liquidator.

Colm Allen was acting for this group of five brokers, just as he had acted so successfully for Frank Murray in the High Court. Just two weeks after getting Murray off the hook, he faxed a report, from which the following extracts are taken. I think you'll agree they make fascinating reading.

On arrival in Gibraltar on Tuesday August 14th (wrote Allen) we had a lengthy consultation with the Hon. Peter Isola O.B.E. who is the senior partner of the legal firm of Isola & Isola. (Peter Isola's chronic gambling addiction was by that time common knowledge on the Rock. Isola's bets of up to £10,000 a day at UK racetracks, his unpaid debts and the visit he received in Gibraltar from British heavies eager to collect the cash he owed, had been the subject of a major feature in the Sunday Times - B.F.) **I was particularly anxious to have the benefit of (Isola's) advice as I knew that he was the attorney who had the liquidator (Gibraltar based) removed in the Irish Trust Bank case some years ago. This was a saga not dissimilar to the one with which we are concerned ...**

Our investigations in Gibraltar have revealed a situation which should not, in my opinion, be allowed to continue. The cost of the liquidation on the basis of a calculation done for us by Mr. Isola now appears to be running at (sterling) £20,000 per week or in excess thereof. At the time of dictating the report Mr Revill is in America with a barrister from Gibraltar, Mr. Peter Caruana. In America he is paying a firm of attorneys to represent him there. The presence of Mr Caruana at very considerable expense is difficult to understand. In addition we understand that (Ronald) Vincent is included in the party. When it is borne in mind that the American properties have long since been identified and that Mr Vincent has had a power of attorney in his possession since February of this year, the purpose of this American trip is hard to understand. One thing that is absolutely sure is that it is further diminishing the funds which will be available to repay depositors.

Ronald Vincent did not accompany Revill to Houston - maybe Colm Allen had been misinformed on this point. Properties were still being identified at the time Allen's report was circulated. The purpose of the American trip was, of course, the freezing of all American assets in Finbarr Ross's name, and as we learnt in Chapter 4 it was a huge success. In August 1984, thanks to the work of Revill, Caruana and Houston attorney Samuel Stubbs, IIL's investors came closer than they ever have since to getting their money back.

Timothy Revill - "extremely good, a professional accountant, on top of things" in the words of Samuel Stubbs - was doing his job well. Too well, perhaps.

Allen's report continues:

We were further alarmed to learn from Mr Isola that the preliminary figure of stg. £4000 per week claimed by Mr Revill while he was provisional liquidator is gravely excessive ... The liquidation is being conducted with scant regard for the interests of the depositors ... there is real reason to question the fees already charged by Mr Revill on the grounds that they are extortionate. Nothing of any consequence has happened since the 19th of June other than the expenditure of large sums of money ... (the) expenditure does not appear to have been justified by results.

As a matter of record, Revill's fees averaged £948.81 per week. The least he earned in any one week was £190; the maximum (for a 55-hour week) was £2,200. Colm Allen evidently didn't consider the matter of the assets tracked down and frozen by Revill worth mentioning. And you may find it interesting that in subsequent reports, the Committee of Inspection did not appear to be unduly worried, and in fact didn't adversely comment on, the fees paid to Declan Collins' firm Stokes Kennedy Crowley. In the year to March 31, 1987, for example, SKC received IR £48,053 in fees from the IIL liquidation.

... the circumstances of his appointment by James Ronald Vincent and the virtual ignoring of the depositors renders him unsuitable for the position ...

Revill was appointed as liquidator not by Vincent, but by the Supreme Court of Gibraltar. His concern for the depositors reflects itself in the regular circulars he sent updating them on how the liquidation was going, and his willingness to work temporarily for nothing in order to recover their misappropriated money. But, wrote Colm Allen in August 1984 (and this is where we get down to the actual objective of his report):

It is imperative that Mr Revill be removed and that he be replaced with another accountant .. I (have) met with Mr Traynor the Treasury Secretary ... preferring not to indicate to (him) at this stage that it is our intention to institute legal proceedings against the Gibraltar authorities for the ultimate shortfall in depositors' funds ...

Those proceedings, to date, have yielded nothing. Allen continued:

I was anxious to enlist Mr Traynor's support for the removal of Mr Revill. At some length I indicated our concerns to the Secretary, mentioning the expense and Mr Vincent's role among other points. I indicated to him that ... it would be my intention to seek Mr Revill's removal and I would expect him to support me to the extent of not interfering. Mr Traynor acknowledged that it was the depositors' right to have their own liquidator and undertook not to interfere in any way.

Colm Allen and Peter Isola had already chosen a likely replacement for Revill - local chartered accountant James Galliano. The report concludes:

I am advised by Mr Isola and believe that we have all the proper legal grounds to justify an application to remove Mr Revill as liquidator and that such application will be successful if sought.

As an example of professional character-assassination, Colm Allen's August 17 report to Frank Murray and the brokers is hard to beat. Clearly, many of the busy young barrister's precious hours had been spent considering how Timothy Revill could be removed from the liquidation. Certainly Allen had found a gap in his diary big enough to enable him to make a lengthy trip to Gibraltar. It makes you wonder whether the legal profession is as time-consuming as its practitioners would have us believe.

It also makes you wonder - how, and why, did Colm Allen get involved in all this?

• • •

The start of August 1984 found me in the seaside resort of Tramore, taking one of my all-too-rare holidays with my family. For a few blissful days, all was peace. Then (you guessed it) the phone rang.

On the line was Liz Maxwell, a fellow private investigator who was looking after my office while I was away. Liz told me 80 confused IIL investors had called the office to say they were being approached by brokers to sign proxies in favour of Colm Allen, on the grounds that Timothy Revill was a crook who was robbing the liquidation of £20,000 a week.

Leaving my long-suffering wife and kids in Tramore - at least they could enjoy the rest of the holiday - I returned to Dublin on August 15. I retained a lawyer in Gibraltar, James Rosada, to attend the creditors' meeting on the 24th and attempt to have it adjourned for three weeks. I needed time to find out what the hell was going on. (Despite his best efforts, James failed in the attempt.)

You sometimes need the patience of Job to do what I do for a living. A good deal of a private investigator's work simply consists of hanging around, waiting, and watching. And, of course, being invisible. I've had many frustrating, fruitless days of surveillance work since I started in this business, and I expect I'll have many more. Days when it's usually raining and I find I'm out of cigarettes. Days when I'm waiting for just one wrong move from my subject to crack a case wide open - but nothing happens.

But I'm glad to say the days between the 17th and 21st of August 1984 were rather more worthwhile. It was then that I staked out Colm Allen, Barry Manning, Frank Murray, Bryan Fryer-Kelsey, and their group of five brokers. I was rewarded with what I would soon realise was crucial evidence.

The following is based on my surveillance reports of that period.

On Saturday August 18, the day after receiving Colm Allen's report, Frank Murray and Bryan Fryer-Kelsey held a meeting with the five brokers at 27 Leeson Park, Dublin (the former address of IIL).

Colm Allen and (solicitor) Barry Manning arrived back from Gibraltar on Sunday August 19. Allen, Manning and Murray met with the five brokers at the Shelbourne Hotel, Dublin, that evening. At this meeting, Allen and Fryer-Kelsey explained to all concerned that they needed to oust Revill ... and that they needed to enlist the support of 15 other investment brokers to collect proxies from creditors in favour of Colm Allen for Friday August 24.

Fryer-Kelsey and a Mr. Noel McKeown disclosed that they had called a meeting of the other brokers for the following night (Monday August 20) at the Ballymascalon Hotel, Dundalk, and that they could count on their support ... They said they could have a 'machine' working collecting proxies on Tuesday August 21 and Wednesday 22, if Allen was able to persuade the other brokers that it was in everyone's interest to get rid of Revill. Barry Manning and Colm Allen agreed to attend the meeting the following night in Dundalk. Murray instructed Fryer-Kelsey to ask one Larry McDermott to assist at the meeting.

Larry McDermott, from Carrickmacross, was Finbarr Ross's former chauffeur. He had also acted as a kind of unofficial broker for IIL, referring 40 substantial deposits to the company from investors in the North, and he was now being put in charge of collecting the vital proxies from depositors.

The plan as discussed at the Shelbourne Hotel (my surveillance report concluded) **was that following the Dundalk meeting the next**

night (Monday August 20), Allen would return to Gibraltar immediately. Barry Manning would stay with Bryan Fryer-Kelsey in Belfast, collect the proxies and join Allen in Gibraltar on Thursday August 23 - the eve of the creditors' meeting - armed with enough proxies to remove Revill.

• • •

I wasn't present at the meeting in Dundalk. I figured I might have been a bit unwelcome. For the details of what happened there, and four days later at the crucial creditors' meeting in Gibraltar, you'll have to rely on the words of Colm Allen.

In a report to Frank Murray and the brokers, dated September 1, 1984, Allen gave his account of the events surrounding Timothy Revill's removal. How did I come by the report? Let's just say I have friends in the most unlikely places ...

The italics are mine.

At the meeting in Dundalk on Monday August 20th, 1984 (wrote Allen) I delivered a report on my preliminary visit to Gibraltar. At that stage I reported in my view the liquidation could in effect be taken over by the Creditors. On Monday night I travelled to London and at 8.45 the following morning, onwards to Gibraltar ...

On Wednesday morning I had a further meeting with Mr. James Galliano, F.C.A., the Accountant I wished to nominate as liquidator in place of Mr. Revill. It should be emphasised that it was essential to our plan that we have a respected local Accountant to act as Liquidator. Without such a person the Supreme Court of Gibraltar would not sanction the removal of Mr. Revill. Mr. Galliano had indicated certain reservations about taking over from a local man in somewhat troubled circumstances. At the conclusion of the meeting, which lasted some two hours, he had agreed, however, to act should he receive the Creditors' nomination on the meeting of the 24th August.

It should be made clear that Mr. Galliano had been retained on the understanding that :-

1. **He would act in the closest co-operation with the Committee of Inspection.**

2. **That every effort would be made to keep the costs of the Liquidation down.**

3. **That the extradition of Mr. Ross to either Jurisdiction would be actively pursued.**

4. **That the role of the Gibraltar Authorities would be thoroughly investigated and the necessary steps taken.**

Point 1 is self-explanatory. On point 2, the cost of the liquidation has certainly been kept to a minimum in the past eight years. This is because since August 1984 activity in the liquidation has also been kept to a minimum. As for points 3 and 4: At the time of writing (September 1992) Finbarr Ross continues to enjoy the good life in Texas he has enjoyed uninterrupted for the past nine years. Not one attempt has been made to extradite him. The Gibraltar Authorities, too, seem to have so far escaped Colm Allen's relentless pursuit of justice on behalf of IIL's investors.

The bulk of the proxies arrived with Barry Manning on Thursday at 1.00 pm. Mr. Manning had remained on to liaise with the Brokers in the collection of the proxies. As the proxies, 410 in all, had to be carefully checked, it was 4.55 pm when we arrived at the offices of the Liquidator ...

• • •

"Allen arrived with briefcases full of proxies", remembered Timothy

Revill in a recent interview. "Later, his and my proxies were counted and he had the vast majority. How did he obtain them? It was obviously a well-organised campaign that could only have come from the brokers - they were the only people with lists of depositors. Allen asked the brokers to go to depositors and prise proxies out of them on the basis that I was ripping them off. Allen must either have told fibs about how much money I was spending, or he was implicitly criticising the Gibraltar courts, who sanctioned all the money spent. He launched a vicious personal attack on me at the first meeting of creditors in Gibraltar - he's a very unpleasant man."

• • •

The Creditors' meeting (continued Colm Allen's report) commenced at 10.00 am on Friday August 24th, 1984. I proposed that the meeting be chaired by Barry J. Manning, Solicitor. J.E. Triay, Senior Partner of the firm of Triay & Triay, Legal Advisors to Mr. Revill, announced that he would be chairing the meeting on the nomination of the Liquidator ... Having asked that my protest as to the choice of Chairman be noted in the Minutes, the meeting then continued with my consent ... It is sufficient to say that the meeting was a stormy one. It lasted in excess of three hours and largely centred around a battle between the Depositors, represented by myself, and Mr. Revill, represented by the Chairman, Mr. Triay.

The representation at the meeting was as follows:-

1. **Colm Allen, B.L., (sterling) £3.59 million.**
2. **Timothy Revill, Stg. £520,000.**
3. **Mr. Marcus Gregory, Stg. £173,000.**
4. **Hassan & Partners, Barristers-at-Law, Stg. £30,000.**
5. **Christopher Finch, Barrister, Stg. £10,000.**
6. **Triay & Triay, Stg. £10,000.**

To summarise, it may be said that Mr. Triay's attempts to control the meeting and protect Mr. Revill did not prove successful.

Two substantiative motions were passed unanimously (with Mr. Revill and Mr. Triay abstaining) being:-

(a) A resolution that an application be made to the Supreme Court of Justice of Gibraltar for the appointment of James P. Galliano, F.C.A., as Liquidator of International Investments Limited in place of Timothy Revill.

(b) That an application be made to the Supreme Court of Justice of Gibraltar ratifying the appointment of -

Colm Allen, B.L.
Marcus Gregory
John Lowe
Bryan Fryer-Kelsey
John Barbour.

Those five men made up the Committee of Inspection. Colm Allen would soon become their Chairman. He recommended to James Galliano that he appoint a chartered accountant with the Dublin firm of Stokes Kennedy Crowley to supervise the Irish end of the liquidation.

Finbarr Ross's former polo-club buddy. Declan Collins.

• • •

On September 17, Timothy Revill swore the following on affidavit to the Supreme Court of Gibraltar.

I am informed by Mr. William Flynn ... that the proxies in favour of Mr. Allen were obtained by a Mr. Larry McDermott of Dunogue, Carrickmacross ... who approached the depositors and ... represented to

them that I had embezzled company funds, paid myself fees of £4,000 per week and employed Mr. Vincent, a director of the Company, at a salary of £1500 per week, thereby implying that I was acting in collusion with the said Mr. Vincent in the defence of private or undeclared interests of his ...

These allegations are injurious to myself and my professional reputation. As stated in answer to a question from Mr. Allen at said meeting (the creditors' meeting of August 24 - W.F.) I paid Mr. Vincent £1500 per month with the sanction of the Court and I have so far received £3,885 to cover the work done and disbursements during the first two weeks of the provisional liquidation ... all subsequent work and disbursements including the cost of travel to Ireland and U.S.A., of myself and one of my legal advisers and of mailing notices to creditors etc., have been carried off and met from my firm's own monies ...

Mr. Barry Manning, who attended the first meeting of creditors as solicitor instructing Mr. Allen and acting for ... Mr. Fryer-Kelsey and Mr. Barbour ... is also the personal Solicitor of Mr. Frank Murray ... Based on the information I have accumulated since this liquidation began it is my personal view that:

(a) This liquidation should not be controlled by the brokers who are responsible for the investment of the public's money in the Company.

(b) This liquidation should not be controlled or influenced by Mr. Frank Murray or any persons associated, appointed or nominated by him or by persons acting for him.

I base these personal views on the belief that such conduct would reflect a serious conflict of interest between those persons and the creditors of the Company.

The representation of creditors by proxy at the First Meeting of Creditors was conducted by Mr. Colm Allen in a controversial manner, which I could not understand or explain, except on the basis that there was a conflict of interests, not disclosed or satisfactorily explained, unknown to me ...

A week later, on September 24, Colm Allen responded to Revill's affidavit to the Supreme Court of Gibraltar with one of his own, which included the following:

... having carefully considered the matters deposed by the said Timothy Revill, it is clear to me that the Affidavit presents an entirely false picture of my own position, that of my solicitor, Barry Manning, and those of my clients. I believe that there are matters relating to his source of information which he has omitted from his Affidavit, thereby presenting an incomplete picture to the Court.

Mr. Revill justified his remarkable allegation of a conspiracy among the brokers by reference to information received from Mr. William Flynn ... the said Mr. Flynn is a private detective who since the liquidation ... has solicited work from depositors ... On Thursday, 23 August 1984, during the course of an informal meeting in his offices in Gibraltar, Mr. Revill discussed Mr. Flynn. Present at that meeting were your Deponent, Mr. Barry Manning, Dr. Marcus Gregory and Peter Isola. During the course of his remarks about Mr. Flynn, Revill indicated that he, Mr. Flynn, was "dangerous" and a "lunatic" ... I am alarmed that in a matter of this gravity he should use the unsupported testimony of one whose bona fides, he has already made clear to myself and my colleagues, are entirely unacceptable to him.

I deny categorically the outrageous allegation that the proxies in favour of this Deponent were obtained by a Mr. Larry McDermott in the manner set out in ... Mr. Revill's affidavit ...

I specifically state that Mr. Frank Murray has no connection whatever of any sort with my clients, nor has he been consulted in relation to these proceedings by me or any depositor or broker. To suggest otherwise, as Mr. Revill does, is to state a plain untruth ...

Allen (and Barry Manning, but not Gregory or Isola) overheard the phone conversation described in the last chapter, in which Revill said that to claim he had been overcharging was "lunacy .. only a madman would suggest that". Timothy Revill has never described me, in an informal meeting with Colm Allen or anyone else, as "dangerous" or a "lunatic". The proxies obtained by Larry McDermott were obtained in exactly the manner set out in Revill's affidavit

As for the relationship between Allen, Manning, Murray and the brokers, I would refer you back to two paragraphs of my surveillance reports for the period August 17 - 21, 1984:

On Saturday August 18, the day after receiving Colm Allen's report, Frank Murray and Bryan Fryer-Kelsey held a meeting with the five brokers at 27 Leeson Park, Dublin (the former address of IIL).

Colm Allen and Barry Manning arrived back from Gibraltar on Sunday August 19. Allen, Manning and Murray met with the five brokers at the Shelbourne Hotel, Dublin, that evening. At this meeting, Allen and Fryer-Kelsey explained to all concerned that they needed to oust Revill ... and that they needed to enlist the support of 15 other investment brokers to collect proxies from creditors in favour of Colm Allen for Friday August 24.'

•••

There follows the transcript of an interview between James Galliano and Sunday Independent reporter Mark Smith, which took place in Galliano's Gibraltar office at lOam on Monday September 16, 1991. Two months after this conversation, Galliano was to resign as IIL's second liquidator.

MARK SMITH : How did you become involved with the liquidation of International Investments?

JAMES GALLIANO : I was approached by my solicitor Peter Isola, who had been instructed (SIC) by a Dublin barrister called Colm Allen. Mr. Isola asked the Supreme Court to appoint me as liquidator.

MS: As far as you were aware, how had Colm Allen become involved?

JG : As far as I was informed, he represented a number of depositors who presumably had gone to him for advice. He also knew people involved in IIL - he had been representing Frank Murray.

MS : Why was Colm Allen so apparently eager to get Timothy Revill removed in your favour?

JG : Mr. Isola said they wanted someone who was detached from the activities of the company. Mr. Revill was too involved. He had been technically managing the company, paying a salary to Ronald Vincent on the Isle of Man. I can't comment further on what was in Colm Allen's mind - the approach came directly to me from Peter Isola.

MS : Why did you appoint Declan Collins as your Dublin agent?

JG : A recommendation by Colm Allen. I knew nothing about Declan Collins at that time, although I knew SKC was a reputable firm. I had no direct contact with Dublin.

MS : Timothy Revill, his solicitor Peter Caruana and Samuel Stubbs in Houston had obtained a six-month freezing order on Finbarr Ross's assets. When you took over the liquidation, did you pursue those assets?

JG : It was done through my solicitors. Mr. Isola and I flew over to the States in January or February 1985. A tremendous amount had been done by Stubbs. When we went to Houston, I got a telex from Stubbs saying most of the assets were worthless - this made it very difficult.

MS : But Stubbs said on affidavit that the U.S. assets weren't pursued.

JG : I have a telex from Stubbs saying the assets were of no value.

MS : Why weren't you in Houston when the "compromise and settlement" deal with Finbarr Ross was signed?

JG : It was something that had been discussed with Declan Collins. He was going to the States anyway for a conference - he said he'd seen what he could get out of Ross to make things easier, and the deal was prepared.

MS : The deal was to have been presented to the Supreme Court of Gibraltar. Why wasn't it?

JG : I refused to sign it. It was a question of giving a "pardon" to Finbarr Ross, saying criminal charges against him would not be proceeded with. I didn't think that was correct. I felt I was not entitled to give any "pardon" to Ross, and anyway it would have been unfair. I felt the whole deal was limiting my powers as liquidator. The agreement was held for a long time at Peter Isola's chambers in Gibraltar.

MS : Did you clash with Mr. Allen and Mr. Collins over the deal?

JG : Not really.

MS : Did you instruct solicitors in Dublin to follow up assets there?

JG : It was done and is still being done by Declan Collins. He has the contact with people there - people he has retained to deal with the sale of assets - but most properties, like those in the States, are valueless, heavily mortgaged.

MS : What about fees paid to SKC?

JG : They were paid for professional services. SKC was trying to trace and prove thousands of loans to individuals and companies. It's sad that a tremendous amount of assets were not realised.

MS : What can you tell me about Billy Flynn?

JG : He has his way of dealing with things, and his approach. He's been over here several times - we've quite recently met. As far as I know he's lost a lot of money pursuing this. How he came into the whole affair I don't know.

MS : He's claimed you've been a "prisoner" in the whole affair.

JG : I'm isolated to a certain extent from the places where events took place. The distance makes it difficult. But I think "prisoner" is an exaggeration. I don't think the fact that I was appointed by Peter Isola at the request of Colm Allen makes me a prisoner.

MS : You tried to resign as liquidator in 1987 - why?

JG : I put my resignation in to the Attorney-General because there were strong indications from Billy Flynn that my appointment was incorrect and invalid. I wrote a letter saying that if the recommendation had been subject to wrongful interpretation, then my resignation is in the Attorney-General's hands. If it's proved at any time that the dethronement of Revill was done for ulterior motives, then I'll resign. If there was any misbehaviour on the part of certain individuals, my appointment would be invalid.

MS : Have you regarded yourself since 1984 truly as liquidator, or just a surrogate of Colm Allen and Declan Collins?

JG : I've always acted as a principle that if things have gone beyond a certain limit - like the agreement with Finbarr Ross - then I've refused to sign, despite Mr. Allen and Mr. Collins suggesting it would be a good thing if I did.

MS : Are you happy with your role in this affair?

JG: No. I wish I hadn't become involved. There's been a tremendous amount of shadow-boxing at times. There've been allegations about my illegal and fraudulent appointment that have been painful. But if I say "I can't continue acting", then I could be indirectly accusing someone of being involved in a fraudulent appointment. I'd be pushing the burden of guilt back somewhere - it's made it very difficult at times to take positive steps.

MS : Do you know what Finbarr Ross is doing now?

JG : I've heard he's in Houston. I'm not quite sure. It's a worrying thing - lots of people have been so badly affected, and there's this question-mark over what happened to the money. The man got a blank cheque in Gibraltar to operate with no supervision. It couldn't happen now.

•••

From Colm Allen's successful coup of August 24, 1984 to the present day, the liquidation of International Investments Ltd has been a low-profile affair.

Most of the investors have given up hope of ever seeing their money again.

Chapter Six

THE DEAL

Fulbright and Jaworski is one of biggest law firms in the world. It has offices in Houston, Washington, San Antonio, Dallas, New York, Los Angeles, Hong Kong, London and Zurich.

It is a law firm with an impeccable pedigree, stretching back to 1919 when the company was founded in Houston, Texas. Today it is ranked among the top five legal outfits in the world in terms of size. Many lawyers believe that when it comes to reputation Fulbright and Jaworski is right there at the top. It retains 700 attorneys, experts in just about every area of the law. Their lawyers are the best; it's a company which can afford to be choosy.

Samuel Stubbs, attorney-at-law, was a partner in Fulbright and Jaworski. For a lawyer, that represented fulfilled ambition: if you worked for F and J, you'd made it. Nobody got there without achieving excellence in his profession.

Samuel Stubbs was, by turns, surprised, baffled and finally scandalised by the circular he was handed one morning.

The circular was from the hand of Colm Allen, Dublin lawyer. It was Allen's report to the Committee of Inspection into the liquidation of International Investments Limited. To Sam Stubbs, the sentiments expressed constituted an insult and an outrage.

The previous liquidator Mr Revill (wrote Allen) retained the services of Fulbright and Jaworski to institute legal proceedings on behalf of the depositors in Houston. That firm has already been paid $25,000 and is now claiming a further $27,000 in order to 'bring them up to date'.

So far it was nothing out of ordinary. A client whining about the high cost of the United States legal system. It happened every day. But there was more ...

Messrs Fulbright and Jaworski are one of the largest and most expensive firms in Houston. Depositors will recall that we were critical of their retention by Mr Revill on the basis that a much smaller and less expensive firm could just as adequately serve the needs of the depositors in this matter.

The person in charge of our case is Mr William Parse. It does appear,

however, that the great bulk of the work is being carried out by a Junior Attorney named Sam Stubbs.

Mr Stubbs does not instil confidence. The proceedings currently in being would seem to be of no use whatsoever to the liquidator, or to the depositors.

What was it that Samuel Stubbs had done, or perhaps left undone, to anger Allen and his friends? Had he overlooked some clever legal way to force Ross to pay up the money he stole? Was he guilty of shoddy work, of failing to follow up leads or take the necessary legal action?

No. It was far simpler. Stubbs was actually getting something done.

• • •

Timothy Revill had engaged the services of Fulbright and Jaworski in July 1984. His urgent aim was to freeze any assets International Investments might hold in the United States before Ross hid them behind his corporate smokescreen of shell companies. Revill knew only too well of Ross's reputation as a financial magician, and realised that if he did not act quickly all IIL's assets in the States might simply disappear from public view.

The American lawyers were retained to instigate litigation against Ross, and to find and preserve any Stateside assets which really belonged to IIL. Ross was, of course, now living in Houston, so a Houston firm was approached to do the job.

Sam Stubbs was assigned to the case, and was briefed that similar proceedings were already underway to secure the Irish and English assets of the company. Revill told him there were strong suspicions that Ross had acquired considerable assets in the States. It was Stubbs' job to find them; no easy task when you are dealing with a man as slippery as George Finbarr Ross.

Revill and his solicitor Peter Caruana told Stubbs that £7 million belonging to IIL investors was as yet unaccounted for, and the logical presumption was that it had been invested in various American ventures under Ross's own name. Stubbs agreed to seek a restraining order and temporary injunction to stop Ross from getting rid of any of those investments, whether they were listed in IIL's own name or indirectly belonged to IIL and its investors.

Fulbright and Jaworski took the case, but immediately warned Revill and Caruana of the possible difficulties they might discover. Stubbs would have to file a lawsuit and obtain bonds for the restraining order and injunction. All this would take time, and in America, like everywhere, lawyers' time costs money. Interrogations would have to be carried out and depositions taken. Fulbright and Jaworski estimated the costs at approximately $100,000, possibly more if a full scale trial became necessary.

They accepted a $25,000 retainer to start the whole business rolling, and Stubbs filed a federal lawsuit against George Finbarr Ross.

It's possible you might now be thinking that $100,000 seems a hell of a lot to pay for the work involved in putting the shackles on Ross. All I can say is that legal fees in the Land of the Free have always been among the highest in the world, and if you want the services of a decent American lawyer - and to trap Ross only the very best would do - then that's what you have to pay.

Of course, they're not much cheaper here. Do bear that in mind, because Colm Allen and the Committee of Inspection would ultimately challenge the sums paid to Fulbright and Jaworski, claiming the firm was too expensive.

Stubbs also prepared an application for a temporary restraining order and temporary injunction. The Federal Court granted the restraining order and set a date for hearing the injunction. Ross was served a citation and a court order requiring him to submit to interrogation and to present himself for deposition - the taking of a sworn statement which can be used in court proceedings in the absence of the witness. So far, so good. Ross was, for the time being, at least, effectively shackled. Now Sam Stubbs had to prepare himself for the gruelling interrogation that was to come.

In early August 1984 Revill and Caruana flew to Houston to go through the files with Stubbs and thoroughly brief him on the intricacies of the case. That briefing took many long hours.

Tracking down Ross's interests in the Texas real estate and oil businesses was no easy task, and Sam Stubbs enlisted the help of a private investigator named Ed Panku from Intersect. Ed is a leading Houston private eye, and Stubbs had no hesitation in recommending him for the job to Revill and Caruana. That recommendation proved well founded. Every day Ed spent on the case, his probings revealed yet more of Ross's Texan empire. There were numerous companies which Ed traced back to Ross, and a multitude of bank accounts. Stubbs explained Ross's ploys for salting away the IIL cash.

"There were no assets held in the name of IIL. What Ross did was to form a limited partnership or whatever each time he did a deal. He would agree to be a joint partner, and to contribute money; but he did not have the money.

"So IIL was not holding the assets. Various shell companies were holding the assets. There were town house developments where for example, the mortgages were worth more than the assets. The general pattern was for Ross to put some up-front money on the table to finance an entire deal in the hope that it would pay for itself. Everything was either in his name or the name of his concern. Any successful project was kept for himself while the loss-makers were put down to IIL."

In mid-August of 1984, George Finbarr Ross finally submitted to make a deposition. The process was intricate and involved, and it took three days to produce the final 574 page document. Throughout this prolonged questioning, Ross made life awkward for Sam Stubbs by repeatedly invoking the Fifth Amendment of the United States' Constitution. That's the one which gives someone the right to refuse to answer any question he feels might incriminate him. I guess Ross had good reason to believe that was exactly what might happen to him if he said too much.

Stubbs recalls his first impressions of George Finbarr Ross.

"He's comfortable, all right. He wears nice clothes, drives a Mercedes and has a nice house on Chevy Chase, the fashionable belt of Houston."

Hardly the hallmarks of a fallen businessman down on his uppers, as some would now have us believe. Despite Ross's belligerent refusal to co-operate, Stubbs, through skillful questioning, did manage to extract a great deal of information and evidence from the ex-boss of IIL.

International Investments' American assets were rarely given any title of ownership which might connect them to those duped investors back in Ireland. They were held under a myriad of names; Pan European Resources

Inc., Balthazar J.V., The Milford Townhomes, Shawnee Exploration Inc., Shawnee Operating Company, Mesa West Partnership, Principium Inc., and many others. As the names reeled out during Ross's deposition, Stubbs dispatched Ed Panku to dig into the background of these shell companies and take a few photographs of what they owned. He was determined to do a thorough job to recover as much money as possible for the cheated investors.

One case Ross actually admitted to on deposition - and remember that's a sworn and legally binding statement - is a typical example of the way he was defrauding IIL depositors. Ross confessed that all the stock of Pan European Resources Incorporated belonged to IIL. He subsequently reinforced this admission when he wrote a letter, dated 16 August, 1984 to Western Bank confirming that IIL owned all of the stock of the company, and that the company should therefore have access to all banking records for Pan European.

Ross had used this company as a vehicle to borrow from Western Bank. As a result, Pan European owed a small fortune to the bank. He also used the company to channel IIL funds into the Shawnee Operating Company or Shawnee Investments Incorporated, another two of his shell companies. In total, $600,000 of International Investments' money went to the Shawnee companies. It was used by Ross to buy ownership interests in a variety of natural gas wells, mostly in upstate New York.

Stubbs told of the way Ross ran his oil business.

"If a well hit gas, the investment was in his name. If not, it was in the name of IIL. Large amounts of loans from Western Bank in Houston represented a lot of dry holes for IIL. By the time that Revill came along, Western Bank were looking for their money."

After the deposition was taken Ross had little option but to agree to a temporary injunction which prevented him from transferring any interest in any property owned directly or indirectly by International Investments.

Stubbs realised that Ross, even under pressure, was a formidable opponent well versed in the art of evading the rules, so another clause was added to the injunction. It prevented Ross from engaging in any transaction of any kind involving $10,000 or more without giving ten days' notice, in writing, to the offices of Fulbright and Jaworski. The injunction was signed by the Federal

Court on 17 August 1984, and was supposed to stay in effect until April 1985.

Furthermore, it was agreed that IIL and George Finbarr Ross would be prepared for trial on March 13, 1985. And that was the closest the crooked Cork financier ever came to facing justice.

On the afternoon that injunction was signed Tim Revill and Peter Caruana left Texas with the 574 page deposition and the knowledge that, for the time being at least, Ross had been stopped.

• • •

During August and September, Revill and Caruana kept in close contact as Stubbs prepared the ground for the trial. By this time I'd become involved with the case, too, and I was helping at the Gibraltar end of the affair, tracking down information and evidence which could be used at Ross's trial.

It was a time-consuming business to untangle the many highly complicated transactions Ross had perpetrated. Whenever my energies flagged I brought an image to mind; the picture Sam Stubbs had painted of the smiling George Finbarr Ross, driving around in his Merc' and living the high life in Texas. He seemed to me like some modern-day Emperor Nero, fiddling merrily on (and the pun here is intentional) while all around him burned. That image concentrated the mind wonderfully.

Stubbs told us that in his opinion - he was the legal expert, after all, and one of the few I've ever had complete confidence in - there was an excellent chance of obtaining judgment against Ross for fraud and conversion, the charges which would be levelled against him under Texan law. But he did have one reservation. He felt he had not yet been given enough time to determine exactly what money would be recoverable from Ross's American interests. He felt, and this was to prove crucial, that because so many different assets had already been uncovered by himself and Ed Panku there was every likelihood he would be able to get the investors "a substantial amount" of their money back.

Stubbs had nothing but praise for Tim Revill and Peter Caruana. "Both Mr Revill and Mr Caruana", he said, "approached the litigation with professionalism and a sense of urgency."

• • •

But then Revill was gone, deposed by Colm Allen's stratagem. Sam Stubbs was understandably surprised, and was given no explanation of what had happened, and no inkling of what was about to happen. On Thursday 27 September 1984 Peter Caruana telephoned him, to introduce the American attorney to the new liquidator, James Galliano.

From that point until early March of the next year Stubbs heard nothing from the new team - Galliano and his lawyer Peter Isola - that would assist or further the looming litigation. None of the expected documentation arrived; no investigative reports were forwarded.

"The new liquidator seldom communicated with me," Stubbs later recalled. "They never paid the money that was due to us. They kept putting us off with statements such as: 'As soon as we've sold the paintings etc. you'll get paid.'"

Stubbs, to use a popular Americanism, was underwhelmed by James Galliano. Just when everything was going their way, things seemed to have ground to a halt for no apparent reason. When Galliano, Isola, Colm Allen and Declan Collins flew out to Houston in March of 1985 the reason became all too apparent. According to Sam Stubbs, Allen and Collins - the real power-players in the game - wanted Ross off the hook.

Stubbs' first impressions of the new liquidator never changed.

"Jimmy Galliano seemed to know nothing. It was confusing to him. He could never keep the facts straight. He did not seem to be in charge. If there was something going on, he did not know. He seemed so out of it. A nice fellow; Galliano was a gentleman."

Stubbs had been told that Declan Collins, an accountant, was Galliano's representative and that Colm Allen headed the IIL committee of inspection. The initial meeting the four men had with Sam Stubbs and his partner Mr Parse proved ineffective. They met several of Ross's business associates, people involved in his American projects, but gained no further insights.

Then Declan Collins, Ross's fellow Polo Club acolyte, met with Ross alone. Stubbs and the others were not invited, and were not told what had been discussed. Other private meetings followed, between Ross, Allen and Collins.

In an interview with Coleman Cassidy of the Sunday Press on October 23, 1986, Stubbs said:

"Declan Collins met alone with Ross for several hours. Neither Mr Allen nor Mr Collins shared any information with me regarding their knowledge of IIL or the activities of Ross. They refused to include me in any meetings with Ross. I was supposed to represent the company in the U.S.A., yet these people would not allow me to meet with Ross or take steps against Ross's interests.

"I was told that Declan Collins knew Finbarr Ross quite well. Declan Collins certainly met with him alone a lot. Colm Allen knew of him ... Allen I found to be a rude, secretive, egotistical guy who behaved suspiciously. He was in charge and everyone else was a fool. He made no effort to work with anybody. He gave an impression of 'I know what's going on - nobody needs to tell me anything'.

"Declan Collins was a little more reasonable. Quieter, but very secretive. He would come out of a meeting with Ross and not tell anybody else what happened."

In April of 1985 George Finbarr Ross, given a breathing space - and, no doubt, fresh hope - by these interminable delays, began his counter-attack. He used an American legal process called "customary discovery". Basically it placed the onus on the new liquidator, Galliano, to get things moving. Galliano was supposed to produce vital documents through his attorney and a date was set for him to make a deposition. He never did either. There seemed to be nothing Sam Stubbs could do to hurry him along.

The "official" excuse for Galliano's non-appearance in America later surfaced, courtesy of a confidential circular sent to investors by Colm Allen on behalf of the committee of inspection. "Regrettably," wrote Allen, "this did not happen ... the liquidator was unable to fly because of a problem with an ear infection."

Did an ear infection lose a fortune for IIL's investors? The real reasons behind all these delays were not long in appearing. They arrived in late April

1985 when Declan Collins made a return visit to the United States and met again with Finbarr Ross and his lawyer Barry Flynn (I'm sure you wouldn't think so for a moment, but I should stress he's no relation of mine). Flynn prepared a compromise and settlement agreement which seemed acceptable to both Ross and Collins. Stubbs recalls Declan Collins asking him to go along with the settlement: "'You've got to give the guy something,' he'd say to me. 'I don't see why,' I'd say. I could not communicate with him on that level. I could not stand Finbarr Ross after what he had done."

Sam Stubbs thought the settlement would help nobody but Ross himself. "I advised Mr Collins that the agreement did not appear to be in the interest of IIL and seemed from the U.S. perspective to benefit only Mr Ross."

That agreement allowed Ross to keep a long list of oil and gas interests in the States - oil and gas interests purchased with the money of IIL's investors. What was more, the only details about where these assets were and who owned what, had been supplied by Ross himself. And it was either Ross, or Ross and Collins together who had placed values on everything. Small wonder that Stubbs disagreed with Declan Collins' judgments about what was best for the company's investors.

"Mr Collins assured me that the agreement was in the best interest of IIL since Mr Ross would be signing over his interests in the Shinrone property in Ireland and since Mr Ross would co-operate in pursuing other IIL principals who may still hold assets. I was asked by Mr Collins to sign the agreement as it purportedly represented the wishes of the liquidator.

"They told me what they wanted. They wanted an agreement that would let Finbarr Ross off the hook."

The deal was not very complicated. It ran to just two pages, and most of the second page was taken up with the various signatures attached. I managed to track down a copy. It didn't make for pleasant bedtime reading. There were damnable catch-all clauses which effectively meant Ross was being allowed to get away with everything. (The all-important Shinrone, incidentally, realised just £18,000 for the investors.)

... the Liquidator agrees, in consideration for the matters described

hereinafter, to voluntarily dismiss all legal proceedings of a civil nature against George Finbarr Ross pending presently in the United States of America, The Republic of Ireland, the United Kingdom of Great Britain and Northern Ireland and the City and Garrison of Gibraltar, and agrees not to initiate any civil proceedings against George Finbarr Ross in any of the foregoing jurisdictions, except to the extent necessary to seek to recover assets, if any, not disclosed on Exhibit 'A'.

Exhibit "A" turned out to be a list headed "Assets Owned By George Finbarr Ross As Of May 1, 1985." It listed what Ross claimed he owned, and his percentage of ownership. According to Sam Stubbs, this unlikely inventory was drawn up purely on Ross's word alone. No attempts were ever made to carry out independent checks on what he said. Personally, I wouldn't trust George Finbarr Ross to tell me the right time, but Declan Collins appeared willing to take his word even though it was obvious how much Ross stood to gain by concealing his interests.

Stubbs recalled with horror his first sight of the settlement and list:

"It went something like this: '25 percent in my (Ross's) name; 25 percent in IIL's name. I'm willing to throw in a share of this...' and so forth. Collins, Allen and Ross divided up the properties and let Ross keep all the oil and gas holdings. The settlement never was consummated, however. They were to go back and have it formally ratified in Gibraltar, but this was never done."

The agreement was - for IIL's investors - a classic example of something not worth the price of the paper it was written on. But it certainly proved of some value to Ross. By the time the deal had been finished time had run out. The injunction had expired. Galliano had not responded to the various requests made on him, and on top of that the Federal Court was now threatening to throw out the lawsuit against Ross. Without support from the men he was supposed to be representing, Stubbs had little option but to abandon the suit. "The lawsuit could not have been won without full co-operation and enthusiasm on the part of the liquidator. You can't try a lawsuit in the U.S. without witnesses and documents from Ireland and Gibraltar.

Stubbs attempted to save at least some of the money for the depositors of International Investments by trying to make sure that shabby agreement was officially ratified. But even this was never done.

"I kept telexing: 'Where's the deal?' I'd had to submit the 'settlement' to the court or have my case dismissed. The Federal Court was threatening to dismiss my lawsuit as I was not prosecuting. And without the settlement being ratified, I could not pursue my case in the Federal Court. I kept telexing them to pay my fees - my partners in the firm were not exactly pleased, I knew, at the way this business had turned out, and I felt responsible to them: 'Pay my fees and let the conversion of the assets as per the settlement get under way.'"

Stubbs kept on sending telexes; his only answers were placatory messages from Peter Isola advising him the committee of inspection approved the settlement and that all was proceeding smoothly. And sure enough, the Committee of Inspection made sure Galliano proceeded smoothly ... to do nothing. In the words of Sam Stubbs:

"In the event the Federal Court threw out the proceedings and Ross walked off, scot free. I blame this on the failure to have the settlement ratified or more importantly on the failure on agreeing to any kind of settlement. I went along with this settlement, because it might mean saving some of the depositors' money and because that's what my client (Collins) ordered."

The Federal Court eventually dismissed Stubbs' lawsuit against George Finbarr Ross in January 1986. It was the closest Ross would ever come to facing trial.

•••

Sam Stubbs had not realised what sort of men he was up against.

While all this legal back-pedalling was going on, Colm Allen was busy behind the scenes, smearing his name and reputation to the investors so they would not place any trust in anything he said.

One of the main accusations Allen was making was that Stubbs' firm, Fulbright and Jaworski, was charging far too much money, an amount which simply wasn't available to pay. In reality, as I discovered through my own investigations, the money was there for the taking to pursue the case through the American legal system the cash had been pledged by the Gibraltar government.

Declan Collins told Stubbs there was no more money to pursue the case. But Collins and Colm Allen had not called on the $75,000 loan arranged by Revill from the Gibraltar authorities. I decided to give Stubbs a call and let him know the true facts behind what was going on. Sam Stubbs, I felt, had been a victim of the notorious "mushroom" treatment - he'd been kept in the dark and fed only on manure.

I also questioned quite what role Collins, a chartered accountant, albeit a rather high-powered chartered accountant, was playing in the game. What on earth was the Irish agent to Galliano doing in America? It should surely have been normal practice, and sound business sense, to retain a Houston-based accountancy firm. Declan Collins' company even had a branch office in Houston. Both Stubbs and I could only speculate why he had not taken advantage of their convenient location and presumable expertise with the intricacies of the American real estate market.

I was pressing Stubbs to swear an affidavit about everything that had gone on at the Houston end of the International Investments affair. This would have been of enormous help in actions I was bringing to replace James Galliano with an effective liquidator who would represent the investors' interests. But once Declan Collins learned what I was doing, and found out I'd-been in contact with Sam Stubbs, he started gunning for me, too.

Perhaps Collins wanted Stubbs to close the file on IIL and get out of the case. And I was rocking the boat. Collins sent a letter to Stubbs accusing me of being a madman - now where had I heard that one before? Fortunately for me, and maybe for IIL's investors too, Sam Stubbs ignored it. He did swear an affidavit, not entirely on my account, but because he believed that if he didn't he would be reneging on all the principles of justice he had worked for throughout his whole career.

Colm Allen, meanwhile, had continued to pressure the depositors with stories about the "overpaid" Yank. In March 1985, under some pressure himself from the creditors to explain exactly what had gone "wrong" with the those American proceedings which originally seemed so hopeful, Allen sent out a circular as Chairman of the Committee of Inspection. It was little more than a smear.

Mr Revill retained the services of Messrs. Fulbright and Jaworski to institute legal proceedings on behalf of the depositors in Houston," explained Allen. "That firm has now been paid the sum of $25,000 and is now claiming a further $27,000 in order to 'bring them up to date'. Apart from that expenditure the private detective engaged by them has to date been paid some $5,000.

Messrs Fulbright and Jaworski are one of the largest and most expensive firms in Houston. Depositors will recall that we were critical of their retention by Mr Revill on the basis that a much smaller and less expensive firm could just as adequately serve the needs of the Depositors in this matter. The person in charge of our case is Mr William Parse; it does appear, however, that the great bulk of the work is carried out by a Junior Attorney named Sam Stubbs.

Mr Stubbs does not instil confidence. The Proceedings currently in being would seem to be of no use whatever to the Liquidator, or to the Depositors.

Colm Allen went on to give his own account of what was happening across the Atlantic. Ross, he claimed, was "certainly short of cash".

We think an enormous amount was achieved by the trip to Houston. A great deal more work remains to be done and it will be necessary to return to Houston within the next few months in order to complete the work which has already been got under way. The liquidator has at all times been very wary of expending depositors' money on expensive trips in circumstances where the assets are so small. The visit to America, however, has

established beyond contradiction that it is considerably cheaper for our representatives to go to America and do the work than to harness the somewhat expensive facilities offered by Fulbright and Jaworski.

Cheaper, as it turned out, for Declan Collins and Colm Allen to let Ross off the hook than for Sam Stubbs to bring him to justice. Allen also claimed in that circular that the depositors would be lucky to see much return from Ross's assets in America if the legal proceedings did go ahead, and mentioned a "realistic" figure of between £6-700,000 at best. It was a very different estimate to Tim Revill's and - when one considers the only real evidence behind that figure was Ross's word itself - a highly imaginative one. It was a figure conjured up out of the need for a bit of psychological brainwashing.

That brainwashing - the efforts to persuade the investors their money is as good as gone - still goes on. The public stance of the committee of inspection is neatly summed up in a few lines from a committee report, again from the pen of Colm Allen, on the eve of a depositors' meeting in June 1986.

The pain and anger experienced by most depositors at the loss of their money has been greatly heightened by the stories appearing (and still appearing) which suggest that Finbarr Ross disappeared to America with somewhere in the region of-£5 million to £7 million. To lose one's life savings is bad enough. To do so and to suspect or to be told that the person who stole those monies is living the 'life of Reilly' in America is to add insult to injury. Your Committee is anxious that you should know there is no truth in such stories.

The very nature of the fraud which was perpetrated by Ross made it impossible for such monies to exist ... The Committee is most anxious that this myth of the 'missing £7 million' be laid to rest once and for all. Its existence greatly adds to the heartbreak and anguish suffered by individual depositors and makes the work both of the liquidator and the Committee practically impossible. No such sums exist and the depositors will have to look elsewhere for such redress as they may be able to obtain.

Here's another example - I reckon it's a much better one - of adding "insult to injury". At the time investors received that controversial summary from the committee, they were told that if they wanted to see the "official" report on what had happened in ~ America it would cost them an extra £2 each. As if they hadn't lost enough.

This story, that there was simply no money in America, is still paraded around today. I've no idea how the flamboyant Mr Ross has managed to finance his extravagant lifestyle in the six years since Colm Allen assured the investors: "There is nothing within the Company (IIL) which would pay back a single depositor a single penny of his investment." Perhaps Finbarr has come up trumps on some national lottery.

And I can't help wondering how Allen and Collins felt so confident in their summary of those American assets, since the only known probing was done by Revill, Stubbs and Ed Panku. They all felt Ross had something he was desperate to hang on to.

But if Ross told his old Polo Club friend Declan Collins that he was skint, during those meetings behind closed Texan doors, who are we mere mortals to argue?

•••

Sam Stubbs was off the case. No doubt certain people hoped that was the last they would ever hear of him. But three years later, in 1988, his name was to figure again.

I hoped that at least some good would come out of all the hard work Stubbs put into the International Investments affair. As far as I was concerned, his affidavit, which set out exactly what had happened in Houston, was extremely enlightening. It constituted firm evidence from one of the partners of the fifth largest law firm in the world about the way Declan Collins and Colm Allen struck a deal with Ross, and excluded their own attorney from that deal.

Stubbs, I reasoned, would be my star witness in a case I was taking in Gibraltar on behalf of the investors to try and remove Galliano as liquidator and replace him with somebody who might get something done. I re-read his affidavit. All the facts were there; from the secret meetings to the description of Galliano's non-role in those Texan discussions. But once again Stubbs' testimony was to be blocked.

I got the bad news through my lawyer's agent in Gibraltar, Haresh Budhrani. The Committee of Inspection was claiming Stubbs' evidence was inadmissible, on the grounds of "lawyer and client privilege". If it had not been so tragic, the very idea might have been laughable. What sort of "clients" were they that refused to let their lawyer take part in meetings with Ross, and failed to inform that lawyer about what happened in those meetings? There was certainly an unfortunate irony in the stance the Committee was now taking. Haresh's letter made it clear that as far as the Committee was concerned, anything Stubbs once said was now just ancient history.

In my view...it is quite likely that the Court would rule Mr Stubbs' evidence inadmissible and, indeed, I am reluctant to put Mr Stubbs' professional standing in jeopardy without having discussed the matter with him thoroughly, bearing in mind particularly Mr Isola's threat to report the matter to the professional body of which Mr Stubbs is a member.

When he discovered what was happened, Stubbs was irate. He had been threatened and his evidence snubbed. If he wanted to be heard at all, he had little recourse but to speak to the press. He told one paper:

"My contact with my new clients was minimal and so suspicious; so unlike what an attorney-client relationship should be. Under our code of ethics, if somebody attempts to include an attorney in fraud, any obligations of professional privilege are waived.

"I'm not saying it is fraud, but it sure don't pass the smell test."

Samuel Stubbs and Fulbright and Jaworski, incidentally, are still waiting for full payment of their bill.

Chapter Seven

A QUIET RAGE

I confess to being stubborn. I may even be obstinate. From time to time I'm accused of being cranky, awkward, wilful, a little obsessive, occasionally intractable. Even, when the mood takes me, completely unmanageable. I'm unorthodox, sometimes undiplomatic and often uncooperative. (There are several prominent Dubliners who would tell you I'm quite unspeakable.)

But there is one thing I'm not. I'm not mad.

• • •

Frank Kelly rang on May 26, 1984. It was a Saturday. It was also the weekend. And that, as the Americans would have us all saying, is "quality time". Frank didn't find me in receptive mood. He may well have mentally added a few more negative traits to the list above. Like impolite. Uncaring. Unhelpful. Downright rude. It was a Saturday. I shouldn't have been in the office at all. Weekends were for the family. I told Frank to get stuffed.

But Kelly was persistent . He kept on calling. I began to dread the ringing of the phone. I would have left it off the hook, but when you're self-employed you just never know ... it could always be The Call, the one that makes your fortune. Frank Kelly's call certainly wasn't.

Each time he rang (and before I could get him off the line with maximum speed and minimum tact) he managed to tell his unwilling listener a little bit more of the story. Frank Kelly was from Birmingham, an ex-pat Irishman in the building trade. He'd invested his money, he said, and had lost it. I said goodbye and hung up. I'd been in the same boat myself, and knew from bitter memory how little could be done for a duped investor. Besides, he'd lost his money. How could he afford to pay me? Too many people think of private detectives as charity workers.

Saturdays have a habit of dragging on. The office is empty. There's an almost unreal quality about working in the vacuum of inactivity. You get easily distracted and start daydreaming, noticing things. Like the dust hanging in the air, the overflowing ashtray (on weekdays it just seems to empty itself) and the slow, muddy passage of the Liffey, dominating all angles of view from the office windows ...

... and the paperwork waiting to be done. A mountain of loose- leaf bloody folders. Whoever invented paper has a lot to answer for. I wished I could grab the whole bundle, hurl it from the window, watch all those hated A4 sheets flutter down into the river. Saturdays. No-one around, and no-one to share a drink when you get bored. Which is exactly what I was, tunnelling away at that lurking loose-leaf mountain; filing is not the greatest of my joys. I guessed Philip Marlowe would have had his own filing clerk. (Not that I usually read detective stories ... they always seem to be about a completely different profession, where the humdrum routine of investigation is replaced by dangerous stake-outs and deadly shoot-ups. And they never seem to star a family man from County Meath in the leading role.)

The phone rang again. A healthy, old-fashioned ringing, not the castrated warble of some modern designer-trimphone. And once again it was Kelly. He'd already distracted me a couple of times to the point where I couldn't concentrate on the work, so I lit another Rothmans and sat back to listen. I'd give him a little longer this time. Frank had invested £7,000, his life savings, in a Dublin-based company called International Investments. Now that money was gone. Could I get it back for him?

No. I hung up again. I'd been stung that way myself, when I'd invested ten times that sum in a building company, and had been embezzled out of it all. I'd been a car dealer then, a man from the motor trade. The overnight vanishing act of my £70,000 set me off on a different career. When I'd seen how the establishment closed ranks to protect itself, I'd experienced a quiet rage, a certain knowledge that there was something rotten in the world; but maybe, just possibly, I could do something about it. It sounds a bit altruistic, but that's how it was. And that, indirectly, is how I became a private detective.

Chance threw that career-change at me; the combination of my new-found feelings of injustice and frustration, and the arrival of a letter.

I'd been discussing my case with Brendan MacLua, the editor of the Irish Post in London. Just in passing, he mentioned to me the plight of a young Irish girl living in the British capital who'd just written to him. Like me, she too had been duped by the system.

She was 17 when her life fell apart. She'd been holidaying with her mother's folks in County Donegal. One evening, coming home from a dance, a local businessman crashed his car into the one in which she was a passenger. She went through the windscreen. Forty stitches and severe facial scarring. Her mother had been to see a local solicitor to find out what action could be taken. Photographs were taken of the girl's face as a permanent record of the damage. By all accounts, they weren't a pretty sight. It should have been a straightforward insurance claim.

In time, the girl came out of hospital and set about the awful task of facing the world with her injuries. She'd had plastic surgery, too, and that would take months to heal fully. She returned to London. Nothing more was heard from the solicitor.

Next summer, back again in Donegal for the summer holidays, she went to his office. "Don't worry," he told her, "these things take time." Naturally she believed it. You tend to believe a solicitor in much the same way you would your doctor or dentist. But years went by and still nothing happened. Eventually, in desperation, the girl changed solicitors, only to find that when the file was requested it appeared to have been "lost". The photographs, too, were missing. It turned out no insurance claim had ever been registered against the guilty party. The time limit for such a move had expired years ago.

Something in that girl's story struck a chord. I, too, had been the victim of legal trouble. I told Brendan I would see what I could do to help the girl. Me, a Meath car dealer. He must have thought I was talking crap.

Some people are destined to their particular careers and professions. Doctors and lawyers seem to head off on their chosen paths without a moment's doubt. Their life is mapped out for them; they know damn well they were never meant to become plumbers or carpenters. I became a private detective by accident. Years in the motor trade, and then one chance phone call set me on my way. But I knew then, as I sorted out that girl's problems in Donegal, that I'd found the right career.

At first I wasn't too enthusiastic about accepting the fact. I was a reluctant private eye. The fledgling Sam Spade would far rather have been

Top - Eileen, Andrew and Clare. (Family photograph)

Bottom - November 1991, Tim Revill briefs Tim Clunie on the affairs at the Caleta Palace, Gibraltar.

Top - September 1991, Gibraltar, L to R, Stewart Hunter, Tim Clunie, Oliver O'Sullivan and Billy Flynn.

Bottom - Desmond O'Malley leader of the P.D.'s & Dick Spring leader of the Labour party.

Top Colm Allen at the Beef Tribunal.

Bottom - Elio Molocco who purchased from the liquidator of Shellmar Holdings (I.L.L. subsidiary) a site at Aungier Street and overnight made a £227,000 profit. Mr. Molocco was also solicitor to the Irish Press.

Top - Peter Isola, Declan Collins and James Galliano in Gibralter. Far left Colm Allen is hidden by Peter Isola.

Bottom - Liam Lawlor, T.D. for Dublin West.

Left to right: daughter - Eileen, son - Peter, daughter - Claire, son - Andrew, my wife - Eileen.

NEWS
LETTER

International Investments Limited.

Leon House, Secretary's Lane, Gibraltar.
Telephone 2346. Telex 2274

SHOULD YOU REQUIRE ANY FURTHER INFORMATION PLEASE CONTACT US DIRECT
OR THROUGH ANY OF THE FOLLOWING:

Nuala Hussey
27 Leeson Park
Dublin 6
Tel: 974269/974258

Larry McDermot
Dunogue
Carrickmacross
Co. Monaghan
Ireland

Kevin Logue
35 Weston Park
London N8 9DE
Tel: 340 2646

Or your Agent

Top I.I.L.'s News letter.

Bottom Michael Mcdowell, Chairman of the P.D.s.

Top - Mary Harney, Junior Minister, whom I met during 1977. She promised a meeting, but was received with a deafening silence.

Bottom left - John McHale, an investor at his Manor Park home.

Bottom right - John McHale pictured on the proposed site, where he planned to retire.

Top - Tim Revill

Bottom - The disappointing response I received from the Gardai

AN GARDA SIOCHANA

Any reply to this communication should be addressed to:

Commissioner,
Garda Síochána,
Phoenix Park,
Dublin 8.

and the following number quoted:

C25/120/85
612D/89/BD/AW.

OIFIG AN CHOIMISINEARA,
BAILE ÁTHA CLIATH.

GARDA SIOCHANA
DESPATCHED
26 OCT 1989
CRIME BRANCH

Mr. William Flynn,
Rathcore,
Enfield,
Co. Meath.

Dear Mr. Flynn,

RE:- INTERNATIONAL INVESTMENTS LIMITED.

I refer above and your telephone call to the undersigned on the 26th inst.

Investigation File in the above matter was submitted to the Director of Public Prosecutions who directed that no person should be prosecuted.

Yours faithfully,

SUPT.,
(F. GLACKEN) for A/C.

back on the car lot, selling perfect, faultless secondhand Nissans to eternally delighted customers (that's my story and I'm sticking to it). But Brendan did me the honour of publishing a small article in the Irish Post about my success with the negligence case, and it was as if the floodgates suddenly swung open.

Letters began to arrive. At first in dribs and drabs, and then in their hundreds. The Irish community in Britain, it seemed, all had a tale or two to tell about negligence, trickery and deceit. For a while I did my best to dodge the cries for help and pleas for assistance. I handled a couple of cases as a favour to Brendan who, in return, published another article saying I was not available for any more work. It didn't seem to make a jot of difference. My profession had been decided for me.

For years I did much of my work among the Irish community in Britain. I held regular surgeries every fortnight at the Irish Centre in Murray Street, just off London's Camden Square. The Centre was run by the Oblate Fathers, who many years before had been responsible for educating the young Billy Flynn at Belcamp College in Malahide, North Dublin. Now I had grown up, and my former teachers let me use their London premises free of charge. That's true Christian charity.

But it was an odd site for such an endeavour. Just around the corner, in the Square itself, the city's monied trendies - the film directors and actors - led pampered lives behind the stuccoed facades of their elegant Georgian homes. And there at the Centre I sat behind a battered desk and listened to countless stories of treachery and dishonour from the world of the Other London; the building sites and road gangs.

In case this is making me sound like some sort of missionary, let me say here the experience didn't turn me into a philanthropist or a do-gooder, but it did teach me one thing about injustice. I learned to despise it. And, when the fates were smiling, to beat it.

I also learned I possessed the single most vital tool of the private eye's trade; tenacity. I was prepared to go on knocking on the same doors time and again until something got done. By being a little bull-headed, I found, you eventually got those doors to open. Even the mighty bastions of the legal establishment weren't so impenetrable if you knew where the key was hidden. Gradually I lost my awe of lawyers and the privileged elite they belonged to. The world of high society was only an obstacle if you yearned to join it yourself. Billy Flynn, the car dealer-turned-detective from Meath, had no such pretentions.

As the procession of the wronged filed past my desk in Camden Town I learned of the endless permutations and motivations that go to make up human nature. Sure, there's good and bad, but there's a million different levels in between. That's something the law cannot hope to realise; that morality too has its class structure. Grasping this fact is essential education on the private detective's syllabus, for without that knowledge you can't begin to make accurate judgments about people and the things they do.

(Sometimes it seems there's a kind of natural law at work here, that the higher up the social scale someone is, the more dubious their ethical code. Maybe I'll add a few X's and Y's and write it up as an equation ... Flynn's First Law of Morality ... they could teach it at law school.)

Four years of investigation had passed by the day Frank Kelly dialled my number and changed my life. I'd become successful at my work, and developed something of a reputation for myself as the man to turn to in the last resort. When all else seemed to have failed and bleak crisis loomed, try Billy Flynn. Often it worked. That's exactly the position Frank Kelly was in; he felt he'd reached the end of his tether.

I'd like to be able to look back and say it was my heart of gold which finally persuaded me to put the case of International Investments on my files, but I'd be lying. Frank, despairing of ever drumming any sense into my head, called a mutual friend. It was he who twisted my arm and made me take the case.

• • •

Liz Maxwell and I aren't exactly in official partnership in my detective firm, Zimmerman and Company, but we do have a working arrangement. Like myself, Liz is a private eye - one I rate very highly indeed. We split up the workload. I admit it's an uneven division; I take the jobs I want and Liz deals with the matrimonial cases. That's not really my scene. There's nothing immoral in the work, but I'd just as soon somebody else did it. It depresses me.

Cases of that sort which fall my way I pass on to Liz. In return she sometimes helps out with my side of the business. So when I went with Eileen and the kids for our summer holiday to Tramore in County Waterford, I left the office in Liz's capable hands. If anything important came up she would know what to do. And if anything really serious came up, she'd know where to find me.

International Investments has a habit of interrupting my private life. On Saturday, August 11, 1984 - these things always seem to happen on a Saturday - I was in Tramore, peacefully buffered from the worries and stresses of the business. I'd taken Frank Kelly's case on board and, over the past few months, had done what I could to find out exactly what was happening in the liquidation, and the roles being played by Colm Allen and his colleagues.

Any initial doubts I'd had about Tim Revill had long since been replaced by a growing confidence in his ability to get Frank and the other investors their money back. I was keeping tabs on what was happening at home in Ireland, and in Gibraltar and the States. Then, once again, a phone call brought bad news.

When I got back to my hotel for lunch there was a message to call Liz at the office. Something pretty drastic must have happened for her to risk interrupting my vacation and bringing the full fury of Billy Flynn's wrath down on her head.

When I returned her call, Liz was apologetic, but in no mood to put up with one of my bumptious tirades. Liz had troubles of her own. She was under siege. The Zimmerman phone hadn't stopped ringing all day. At the latest count, 80 of International Investments' depositors had called, all with the same story. They were confused by what had just happened. They'd been contacted by their investment brokers seeking proxy votes in favour of one Colm Allen. There were differences in the tales the brokers had used to support this request, but one strand seemed fairly common. Tim Revill was, they said, a crook who was robbing the liquidation of £20,000 a week.

Liz, who's no slouch in any aspect of the detection game, had done a bit of digging of her own. She believed there was a written report circulating, signed by Colm Allen, which revealed information on what was being said about Revill. I asked her to try and get hold a copy and she said she would. I knew there was an important meeting of IIL's creditors coming up and I wanted to have a full grasp of the facts before then.

I decided to break one of Billy Flynn's Ten Personal Commandments and let work cut into pleasure. The following Wednesday I returned briefly to Dublin.

As I drove north, I thought back to that first meeting with the formidable Mr Allen, in the Four Courts just a few weeks previously, after Tim Revill got his interim injunction against International Investments in Ireland, to stop what assets there were from disappearing. On Monday July 30 the matter was scheduled for a full hearing. Monday July 30, the day Colm Allen first put the fear of God into me.

I had been sitting in the back of the courtroom, shaking my head with disbelief at what I was hearing. I've already mentioned my dramatic interruption of the proceedings. I ought, perhaps, to explain the effect Colm Allen had on me that day. When he applied for the whole proceedings to be dismissed against Frank Murray, I just couldn't believe it. Frank Murray was the man who'd actually signed his name as IIL's chairman. Surely this wasn't justice, however loosely you choose to define the word. It was all so unexpected, and it was happening so fast. Somebody had to try and do something.

I've admitted before that when I reckon something important is at stake I don't stand on ceremony. It's as if there's a little click somewhere inside my brain, a switch that sets me running on automatic pilot. And it doesn't seem to matter if I happen to be somewhere where I really ought to be behaving myself. Frank Murray was getting away with it in front of my own eyes, and the switch clicked.

I was on my feet. Everyone's eyes were staring hard. Staring at me. And the look in Colm Allen's eyes ... I'd have to describe it as chilling. In short, I was making myself unpopular again.

My outburst did have some effect. Colm Allen had been forced to reply to what I said, and lost little time in turning defence into attack. William Flynn's allegations, he told Justice Keane, were entirely groundless. Furthermore, Flynn held no retainer in this case, and should be held in contempt of court. (The way Colm Allen said this, the phrase seemed to have an almost palpable edge of menace. Perhaps I'd be more accurate if I described it with capital letters - Contempt Of Court. Not something I particularly want to be held in, then or ever.)

Justice Keane let the matter rest, explaining that in view of the fact that I wasn't a named party in the proceedings he could not entertain my comments, and certainly would not allow my application. Crisis over; William Flynn remained at liberty, but with nothing achieved. Justice Keane summed up, then said he was going to grant Colm Allen's application. The switch clicked again and Billy Flynn, private detective and inveterate courtroom pest, was on his feet once more, interrupting the smooth running of the process of law.

Couldn't Justice Keane consider even an adjournment of the hearing, I pleaded? Then I could at least brief Tim Revill's lawyers on certain issues. Like the best way to stop Murray getting off the hook. Not a chance. Colm Allen stepped in again, once more suggesting I be held in Contempt Of Court for my incessant pesterings. Fortunately for me, Justice Keane declined what must have been a tempting suggestion - to provide me with bed-and breakfast accommodation in a Gardai cell. I managed to walk out of the courtroom with my freedom still intact, and sat down outside Court Two, waiting to catch a word with Revill's lawyers. I could at least let them know what I had been trying to do, and make some explanation for my unseemly behaviour. That first brush with Colm Allen had left me shaken, and I needed someone on my side.

Vincent O'Neill walked up. Vincent, I knew, was from Carthy O'Neill, Tim Revill's Irish accountants. What's more, I knew by reputation that he was a trustworthy man, one of the most highly respected chartered accountants in Dublin. When he approached me and said it was obvious I knew something Revill's team did not, I had no hesitation in setting up a meeting to tell him exactly what it was. My little outburst had at least earned me something; an ally.

• • •

Back in Dublin from Tramore, I spoke to Liz and soon realised I needed a lawyer in Gibraltar to go to that creditors' meeting and represent my clients' interests. After much ringing around I tracked down someone I felt I could trust, a solicitor named James Rosada. I asked James to go to the meeting and try to get it adjourned for three weeks. In the event, his application was refused, but I wasn't to know that as I drove back to Eileen and the family in Tramore.

Holidays were over for me the next Saturday, and from that day until this I haven't had a clear break from the sordid shambles the IIL affair was to become. Monday morning in the office brought another call, this time from Vincent O'Neill. I'd been wise to take him into my confidence; he was proving a useful contact. His news, however, appalled me. Tim Revill had been dismissed.

Something had to be done, and quickly. The cartel's backstage politicking was now public. Without Revill we were back to square one. Or possibly worse. I wondered again at the sheer arrogance of men who felt they could just twist the system whenever it suited them. But of course, the sort of people I was dealing with knew they could. Five men and true sat on that Committee of Inspection, but how many of them were really pulling the strings?

I called a meeting, intending not just to put a brake on what seemed to be happening, but to put an almighty fear of God into the cartel's members. The list of people attending would surely make Allen and Co. sit up and take notice for once. Detective Ryan of the Fraud Squad, a representative from the Register of Friendly Societies, Michael Meagan from Arthur Cox and Company - the Dublin- based agents of Tim Revill's liquidation. Vincent O'Neill came along, too, with fresh information.

Since I'd last spoken to him, O'Neill had been contacted by Declan Collins. Collins informed him he was dismissed from the liquidation, and that Collins himself had been appointed in his place. Would he be kind enough to send on the relevant paperwork? O'Neill told us he hadn't yet done so, but had instead called Revill in Gibraltar. Tim Revill had explained he was planning to file an affidavit in the Supreme Court of Gibraltar about the manner in which he was removed from the job.

It was a busy gathering; everyone had his point to make. I'd brought along Gordon Hamill, one of the IIL investors and a broker himself. Gordon had been taken for the sum of £25,000 which, in February '84, he'd handed to Frank Murray at 27, Leeson Park, to invest on his behalf. Surprise, surprise - he never saw his money again. Who knows whose pocket, or pockets, it ended up in?

Gordon was pressing me to report Colm Allen to the Bar Council of Ireland. There were calls for politicians to be informed, action to be taken on the floor of the Dail to get the affair out into the public view. Detective Ryan told us the Fraud Squad was conducting an active investigation into International Investments and the men who ran it.

And then, in the midst of all this angry talk, Liz Maxwell - with perfect dramatic timing - put in an appearance. She had yet more revelations for us. Liz explained there had been more behind- the-scenes activity than we'd been previously aware of. Allen had turned up in Gibraltar not just on the 21st, but had been on the island a week before as well. In fact, IIL had given him a busy few days. There had also been the meeting of investment brokers in Dundalk on the 20th, which he had attended with Barry Manning and Frank Murray. Clearly, Colm Allen had already sacrificed a great deal of his valuable time to the IIL affair.

My friend and sometime working colleague John Noland summed up the situation best. He told us the "old hands" had taken control. It was rapidly dawning on me just why Revill had been kicked off the case; he was being too efficient, getting too close to the truth of what had happened in IIL.

• • •

With hindsight, I can now pinpoint the exact moment at which I realised the International Investments affair had stopped being just a routine job. It was on Friday 31 August 1984, the day Liz burst into that meeting. Up until then the IIL investigation had been complicated, but still a normal piece of detective work. There was some background manoeuvring going on, that was for sure, but that's pretty normal in a case like this. Walking back to the office with John and Liz that afternoon the issues became clear to me. This wasn't just a case of financial fraud now, this was something else again.

From September of that year I began to throw all my spare energies into finding out just what was going on with the International Investments liquidation. It was a long haul; it still is. To give you some idea of the extent the case took over my life (and my bank balance) and the resources of Zimmerman and Company, I'll quote, if I may, a few facts and figures.

By the end of 1986 I had interviewed more than 160 people about IIL. The investigation had taken me to five countries; more than 120 companies had been checked out for possible links with Ross and his cronies. There'd been investors' meetings in Cork, Dublin, Birmingham, London and Belfast. I'd kept all the investors fully informed about what I was digging up - that cost a pretty penny, too. The travel alone was costing me an absolute fortune. And then there was the work I was having to turn down so I had enough time to keep the IIL case on the boil. The only payments I'd received to fund all this activity were long since used up. In short, I was skint.

Even by the beginning of 1986 I'd spent £200,000 on the case. I should say here and now that although being a private detective isn't by any means a breadline career, it certainly doesn't give you the sort of income where you can afford to write off a couple of hundred thousand pounds every now and then.

I'd already started borrowing to pay my way and keep the investors' hopes alive. The way I saw it, if I didn't do it then it was bloody certain nobody else would. If I just gave up, counted my losses and decided not to throw good money after bad, that would be the end of any investigation into Finbarr Ross and IIL. Goodbye to seven million quid.

Besides, I had my temper up. I felt I'd been challenged, that there were certain people who imagined I was powerless to do anything about what they were up to. I was being labelled a madman. My efforts were being scorned and ridiculed. My very reputation was being brought into question, and that was something I'd worked long and hard to acquire. No way was I going to give it up now. Not without a fight.

It would not have made sound financial sense to some people, but I decided to borrow my way out of trouble. I knew it was reckless and irresponsible, but what else could I do? In desperation I decided on the last resort; the one I had sworn never to use.

My wife Eileen owned two houses about two miles from the County Meath town of Enfield. On one of them there was still a small mortgage to pay off, but that was almost finished. When it was paid off, our plan was to transfer the house to our eldest son, Patrick. It would be a grand twenty-first birthday present. I knew Eileen had set her heart on this; it's a great thing for a mother to be able to set up her son in his own home with a secure financial future.

I didn't feel too good about what I was asking. My pride damn near vanished for ever. But I really had no other option. I sweated for days, working up the nerve to admit to Eileen what I wanted to do - use both those houses as security to raise more money for the IIL investigation. My wife has the patience of a saint. In fact, if anyone deserves actually to be made a saint it's Eileen. And if someone asks what exactly she did to deserve such an honour, they can be rightly satisfied with the reply: "She put up with Billy Flynn for years." Anyone who's ever known me when times are bad will know exactly what that means.

When the IIL affair dragged me with it through some of my darkest hours, Eileen's support was probably the only thing that kept me going. My friends will tell you that Billy Flynn likes to think he's the tough one. He's not. It's his wife.

I'd already made myself a prime candidate for the title of Least Lovable Husband in the first couple of years of the IIL affair. The whole family would have been quite justified in walking out on me. Black moods; deep, dark depressions; long spells away from the home; interrupted holidays; missed birthdays. And worst of all, the drinking.

I've never had a particular problem with regard to alcohol - I hope to

God I never will - but at those times when the future seems bleak, when I seem to be making no headway at all, sometimes I turn to brandy to help me out. It never lasts, and Eileen knows me well enough to realise that, but it can't be much fun for her never knowing when the hell I'm going to get back from the bar, and what state I'll be in when I do.

And, despite all this, she said yes. I could carry on the fight, mortgage her houses, raise some extra money. I was finally putting the whole family's future on the line.

• • •

Extract from Committee of Inspection report to IIL depositors, December 7, 1984:

William Flynn ... is a businessman who seeks to turn the plight of depositors to his own advantage by extracting fees on the basis of promises which we do not accept can be delivered. Mr Flynn's campaign for business has been conducted largely in the press. It is alarming to us that in articles in which Mr Flynn has featured prominently highly confidential information regarding the business of depositors has been divulged.

We believe Mr Flynn's proposals, if acted upon by depositors, would prove to be disastrous and would seriously hinder the successful conduct of the liquidation.

Extract from Committee of Inspection circular to IIL depositors, December 16, 1987:

The large and representative meeting of 27th November 1987 passed a unanimous vote of confidence in the Chairman and Members of the Committee of Inspection. The meeting also rejected as outrageous the latest batch of lies from Mr Flynn.

I call once again on all Depositors to reject Mr Flynn's malicious and lunatic campaign.

Extract from Committee of Inspection circular to IIL depositors, January 14, 1988:

I am writing to you on behalf of the Committee of Inspection to ensure that Mr Flynn's deliberate attempt to mislead you will not succeed ... Individual depositors may like to enquire of Flynn as to what information concerning their affairs he has reported to the Revenue Commission.

(I have never given any information about IIL's depositors to the Revenue Commission. This innuendo was an out-and-out lie, aimed at driving a wedge between my clients and myself.)

Extract from Committee of Inspection circular to IIL depositors, May 5, 1988:

Your Committee is not going to waste time by going over again all of the lurid and ludicrous allegations which continue to be canvassed by the Flynn party ... Other than the spreading of scandal and the vilification of the Committee of Inspection, what has Mr Flynn achieved?

Malicious? Lunatic? Ludicrous? Words can wound, but I could handle the smears, even such a well-orchestrated campaign of documented attack. But there were other, more terrifying attempts to persuade me to drop the case of International Investments. Threats of a far more sinister kind ...

Chapter Eight

ROCKING THE BOAT

The village of Enfield in County Meath is not, by any stretch of the imagination, in a highly populated area. There are a few pubs and bars, the church, some scattered houses and village shops. It's an isolated region. Only thirty miles from Dublin's city centre, yet sometimes it feels as remote as the farthest-flung corners of Connemara.

The Flynn house is even more out-of-the-way, secluded in a maze of tiny pot-holed lanes and byways. It's cut off - the nearest Garda station is three twisting country miles away - but that's the way I've always liked it. Coming home is more than just a glib phrase to me; it means I can shake the dirt of the city from me, sink into a chair and relax with my family. (And, Eileen would doubtless add, stink out the living room with the foul aroma of a few packets of Rothmans ...)

But while the house is blissfully remote from the stresses of civilisation, it is also completely isolated from its comforts. Like the security that comes from having the Gardai just around the corner, for example. And there were times, during my hunt for the real villains of this IIL affair, when I wished I had the police living right next door.

A private detective knows only too well that the most sophisticated alarm and security systems in the country can't hope to keep out a determined intruder who knows what he's about. Wires can be cut, circuits broken, and even if the whole thing does erupt in a roar of wailing sirens and flashing lights, how soon are the guards going to get there anyway? Which is why I was extremely worried, to put it mildly, when the threats began.

My London secretary, who sorted out cases for me in Britain and arranged my surgeries at the Irish Centre, was the first to pick up the phone and hear its chilling message.

"My name is Simon," the voice began (she thought it was an English accent, but was so shocked about what he said next she didn't really have a chance to register any real details about the voice.)

"Billy Flynn is upsetting people with his International Investments investigation," continued 'Simon'. "If he doesn't ease off he will be in some personal danger. I understand he'll be visiting London next week."

The caller had details, too, of where I would be staying in the British capital, and what I would be doing. He knew my movements. This was evidently not a crank call.

At first, I didn't take it to heart. There have been plenty of attempts to scare me off cases in the past, even a few to buy me off. My secretary, however, was insistent; there was something about the voice, its sharp, terrifying coldness, which had left her genuinely scared for my safety.

So what could I do? I certainly wasn't going to drop the whole business just because the anonymous 'Simon' suggested I ought to. I checked the locks on the doors and windows, did a thorough overhaul of the security system, and thought no more of it. Then the calls began again.

I got them at home and in the office. Eileen, who was far from well at this time, even answered a couple. It was impossible to get any clue from the caller, impossible to trap him into the sort of conversation which might reveal something about his identity, or what he knew. Only one thing was blindingly, shockingly obvious. He knew a great deal indeed about the movements of Billy Flynn. My secretary had been right; this was definitely no nutter. Whoever it was, and whoever he was representing, meant business.

It was impossible to ignore the calls. The phone would ring at all times of the day and night to deliver up fresh threats and menaces. Behind them all was the same message; lay off IIL or suffer the consequences.

I opted for a sensible approach to securing the house, and employed a bodyguard. Like myself, Peter McGilligan was a private detective, and a handy man to have around in a crisis, I knew. I installed him in my company on a full-time basis. Where I went, he would follow. I reasoned that it was far more likely any attack would be on me than on my family.

I never found out who he was, but if I ever catch up with the mysterious 'Simon', he'd better look out.

• • •

Back in 1985 I'd followed up a lead that Liz Maxwell had dug up. She'd heard that a former priest had some involvement - she couldn't find any further information about exactly what sort of involvement - with Finbarr

Ross and IIL. Her information suggested the priest had a number of reports belonging to Colm Allen, which could be useful to us in putting together the story. The priest, she believed, had some sort of disagreement with Allen, and might be willing to let us see those documents. At that time I had no idea at all what those papers might contain - I had my suspicions but for all I knew they might just be his supermarket receipts - but it was something which I felt had to be followed up.

After days of 'phoning around I established the priest might be living in a small village in the French region of Brittany. I even had an address. So I went there. (Trips like this, perhaps, illustrate why an investigation like IIL turned into such a phenomenally expensive business.)

The journey was a waste of time. I found the house, and noticed a few photographs which indicated the priest had at some point been in it, but there the trail went cold. The present occupants of the house were a French mother and daughter, who didn't seem to be willing to give a forwarding address, if they had one, to a private eye from Ireland. There were communication problems, too. I would hardly describe myself as fluent in the French tongue, and conducting an interrogation with a phrase-book in one hand isn't exactly recommended practice.

In the autumn of 1986 I got another chance to get hold of a copy of those documents. By that time I'd learned more about them. They seemed to be reports on how the proxy votes were used at the IIL creditors' meeting which deposed Tim Revill. If so, they'd prove invaluable when it came to presenting the case to the authorities. Up until that point, the powers-that-be hadn't shown much interest, and I hoped some irrefutable documentation might change that.

Liz Maxwell had tracked down our elusive priest. I agreed to meet him in Madrid. I'd been told this man of God wanted money before he was willing to give us a copy of the papers; about £5,000. More costs, and more borrowing to pay for them. I cadged £8,000 from a long-suffering friend, and with my bodyguard in tow set off for Dublin airport.

As we drove north to catch the flight I was suddenly struck by a logical train of thought which really should have occurred to me before. I wanted these documents to use in an official capacity - this wasn't just a matter of getting information to tip off a client. If the priest did insist on cash (doubtless to pass on to some favourite Mission charity) and I handed it over myself, where would that leave me legally? Would I be able to use the documents at all, or would it just be five grand down the drain?

I needed legal advice again. Peter McGilligan wasn't too happy about the sudden U-turn on the Swords Road - too much like a TV car chase for his liking. A top solicitor, Desmond Moran, filled me in on the details. Yes, I'd been right to worry. The reports would probably have less impact if I paid for them. I'd have to think of some way around it.

We flew to Madrid via London, where I met three of the depositors I represented. By now we'd seen so much of each other we had become good friends, which probably helped to reinforce my personal interest in the case. Frank Kelly had forgiven me for my first harsh words to him a couple of years back (although I'm not sure I've forgiven him for getting me involved in the bloody thing in the first place), and John McHale and Tony Morgan were giving me valuable moral support. It was nice to share a drink and talk about International Investments with people who didn't think I was mad.

In Madrid I took a look around while Peter McGilligan checked me into the Hotel Diana; after all, if he was on the payroll he might as well be kept gainfully employed, and no-one actually seemed to be leaping out of dark alleys pumping bullets at me just yet. I doubted that my phantom caller would have taken the trouble to follow me to London and then on to Spain. I took out the notebook where I'd written down the address Liz had given me for the priest. My Spanish is as bad as my French, but it seemed to be some kind of religious address. That made sense; it's not unusual for former priests to go on living within religious orders.

How wrong that assumption proved to be. When we arrived for the meeting an hour before midnight, the address turned out to be a luxury brothel.

There was no mistaking it for anything else. In the ground floor bar there were about eighty girls just sitting around chatting. Most of them didn't have drinks. And these weren't just local girls out on the town for a chat, either. They were, in the words of a Jackie Collins blockbuster, drop-dead gorgeous. Any one of them could have walked straight into the lists of a modelling agency, or breezed her way through a screen test for Dynasty. This was nothing more than a classy whorehouse.

Peter McGilligan, not quite believing my theory, tested it out by asking one of the girls for a light. I was right; the only English they spoke was "one thousand American dollars."

So there we sat, surrounded by dozens of the most stunning women in Spain and their potential customers - mostly middle-aged business types working up Dutch courage. Time passed slowly. The girls had begun to giggle; they probably thought we were just two more embarrassed customers, too shy to approach them. Or too skint. I looked at my watch; midnight. We'd been stood up. Stood up in the middle of a bloody brothel.

But suddenly our priest - the man we had come all this way to see - walked into the bar, and I experienced a sudden flash of recognition. I knew his face. I'd seen it before, in photographs on the wall at that house in Brittany.

I'd already thought of a way around one problem. There was no need for me to pay for the reports and risk them being ruled inadmissible evidence. I had someone with me, my minder. He could hand over the cash, and so long as he didn't tell me what he did with it, how was I to know if the priest had been paid anything? With that in mind I had already handed McGilligan the £8,000 I'd borrowed, and was now using him as a human wallet. When I needed to pay for anything, I got the money from him. I was like the British Royal family; I didn't carry cash.

We shared a few drinks. The priest appeared to be a trusted man at the club, so I just ran up an account at the bar, intending to pay it all off at the end of the evening. And finally those reports were in my hand.

I was so eager to find out exactly what they said I lost track of everything else going on around me. I read quickly but carefully. They were dynamite. They explained exactly what had happened with the proxy votes before the meeting where Tim Revill had been so speedily removed. Just what I needed. Now maybe the authorities might take some notice.

I never found out whether my minder actually handed over money for these documents, and in all honesty I never really wanted to know. I was sticking to the letter of the law. For once the rules were on my side.

And yes, I did pay the bar bill. But not before I'd passed a worried couple of hours in the club. While I avidly scanned the reports, McGilligan had disappeared with the priest for a tour of Madrid's late-night bars. When I finally looked up, he was gone. Leaving me with exactly one Irish pound in my pocket and an astronomical bar tab to settle.

Back in Dublin, after a fruitless stopover in Gibraltar where I achieved nothing except a few nights of fever in an hotel, I handed those reports to the Irish Fraud Squad and the General Bar Council. You'll already have read some of their contents in chapter 5. I hope you'll agree with me when I say that to my mind they're pretty damning.

But did the Irish authorities agree? I might have guessed; they decided to do precisely nothing.

• • •

The rich and exotic nightlife of the Spanish capital wasn't the usual sort of destination the IIL investigation took me to. Most venues were far more mundane. I visited London's Scotland Yard twice in 1985, and also flew to the Isle of Man to talk to the Fraud Squad there about Ronald Vincent's role in International Investments. Each time I got the same answer. They were sympathetic, but couldn't really see how it concerned them. Surely International Investments had been based in Dublin? Why weren't the Irish authorities doing anything about its fraudulent collapse?

I even tried enlisting the services of Interpol to see if they could help, and wrote to their Paris headquarters. Once again, the unwillingness of the Irish authorities to get involved was my downfall; that attempt was overturned as soon as Dublin was consulted. It seemed everyone had an interest in keeping the IIL fraud well away from the headlines.

I tried America's finest, the Federal Bureau of Investigation, sending a report to FBI Special Agent Paul Lorencetti of Houston. He at least took the trouble to ask questions, confirmed what I claimed but said he too was unable to help. The ball was in Ireland's court, and they didn't want to play it.

As my fruitless efforts to twist the arm of officialdom went on I realised that passing the buck was almost an international epidemic among the bureaucracy of law enforcement. Eric Thistlethwaite, Gibraltar's Attorney-General, told me I should get in contact with the police on the Rock.

I did so. Five times - but it all came to nothing. As fast as I latched on to a new contact in a new police department, the word got around. Billy Flynn was rocking the boat. Billy Flynn was stirring up trouble. Get rid of him as fast as you can.

• • •

There were times when I almost gave up. Days when yet another promising effort came to nothing, when the umpteenth door was slammed in my face. A number of my friends added their names to the list of people who believed I was mad to carry on with the case. I dare say Eileen did too, but she kept such thoughts to herself, and I thank her for showing me that kindness. I renamed IIL. To me it was IBI - International Bloody Investments. I wished I'd never heard of it.

But always there seemed to be something, a small glimmer of light, some hope to keep me working away at the puzzle. I now knew exactly what had happened; I'd pieced together all the fragments, and the confusion of those early months was gone for good. I knew the cast of characters like I did my own family; Ross, Murray, Allen, Collins, Vincent - they'd all played their part in the affair, and I now knew what those roles were. I felt like a theatre critic who'd discovered something vitally important about a drama, only to find no-one would take what he said seriously.

Even in this liquidation, the lowest of low-key performances ever staged, there was always something you could do to keep the whole affair from dying. In 1987, three years after Ross's offshore con-trick sank with all hands (apart, that is, from the captain himself) I managed to stir up support for another investors' meeting. And once again, for the Committee of Inspection, it was time to play the proxy game.

I'd given a bit of a jolt to Gentleman Jimmy Galliano by discussing with some of the depositors the possibility of suing both himself and the Committee for negligence. I chatted it over for a while with the investors and we settled on a likely sum of £5.2 million. Not as fantastical a figure as it may seem, because Galliano was by no means an impoverished man. His family had owned their own bank for 100 years (considerably longer than George Finbarr Ross).

It had the desired effect. Word got back to Gibraltar, and it wasn't long before a depositors' meeting was arranged, to be held on the island. Galliano told the press he'd been required to call it to comply with Gibraltar's legal requirements.

"I have informed my solicitors," he said, "and we are certainly calling the meeting as we are obliged to by law."

The imminent meeting pulled me from the doldrums once more. Things seemed to be happening again. Even the authorities were doing something, although not much; the Belfast Fraud Squad had renewed its investigations into IIL.

Jimmy Galliano sensed a change, too. He sold up the family bank. The Phoenix magazine, a keen follower of the IIL liquidation over the years, reported his actions in their issue of October 23, 1987.

The remarkable thing about Jimmy Galliano, banker, is that he has just cashed in his chips, so to speak, by selling the family firm. He did well, too - 'tis said they got between £3m and £4m sterling from Jyske, a big Danish commercial bank. Not bad going at all ...

In fact, Galliano had been prompted by another source to convene that investors' meeting. The Supreme Court of Gibraltar ruled against him when he tried to oppose an action by creditors calling for new, open discussions. My lawyers Oliver O'Sullivan, Stewart Hunter and Haresh Budhrani, who pleaded the action, also called on the Supreme Court to remove Galliano as liquidator, although that part of the case was adjourned. The Sunday Press recorded the court ruling.

"The purpose of the meeting which the Supreme Court has stipulated must take place before January 31, 1988, is to remove the liquidation's Committee of Inspection, comprising a number of prominent Northern Ireland investment brokers and chaired by Dublin barrister Colm Allen ... The action was instigated by private investigator William Flynn and his legal team who claim to hold powers-of-attorney for £3 million of depositors' funds."

And so we did, although once again things didn't go exactly to plan. A date was set for the meeting; Monday, 25 January, 1988, just six days before the legal limit set by the court. Galliano requested all proxy votes to be delivered by the evening of Friday January 23 at 5 o'clock. This, I later surmised, would enable Peter Isola to spend the weekend adding up the proxies on my side, and decide how best to tackle them.

There was the usual pre-meeting runaround by the Committee to gather the proxies they needed to beat me. Insinuations were bandied about that I might possibly be in cahoots with the taxman, and considering many people had placed their money with Ross for the very reason of avoiding tax, that was hardly likely to direct support my way. Like most of these claims, of course, it was absolute, unadulterated, scurrilous nonsense.

Budhrani, my Gibraltar lawyer, suggested it might be a good idea to bring some support with me to the meeting, so I enlisted the physical presence of 23 of the investors, and brought my other legal representatives Stewart Hunter and Oliver O'Sullivan for good measure. We made quite a crowd on flight GT102 from Gatwick to Gibraltar. A fact that can't have escaped the notice of two other passengers on that same aircraft; Colm Allen and Declan Collins. But perhaps they didn't see us. Whereas we were flying economy, they were in Club Class.

Again, I'll let The Phoenix tell the story of what happened. This is from their February 26, 1988, edition.

On the day, the meeting to remove the committee had a distinctly 'High Noon' quality about it. Some 20 hopeful depositors had flown out from Ireland and Britain, advised by their lawyers ... The liquidator took the chair, flanked by his legal advisor, Pete Isola. The colourful

Isola, a member of one of the Rock's most influential families and a former Deputy Chief Minister of the colony, is still talked about in Gibraltar nearly 20 years later as the man whose once promising political career took a one-way nose-dive because of gambling debts.

Colm Allen and John Barbour were present as chairman and secretary respectively of the Committee of Inspection. So too was accountant Declan Collins of Stokes Kennedy Crowley, the liquidator's Irish agent ... Incidentally, the most notable feature of the liquidator's report was that fees of $48,053 were incurred by Stokes Kennedy Crowley for the year to the end of March 1987. And since the only revenue mentioned by Galliano as accruing to the liquidation for the same period was the £82,000 paid to Collins for the sale of Clondalkin shopping centre, it seems that SKC are doing very nicely, thank you.

In the event the depositors' £2.7 million worth of proxies were whittled down to £1.7 on the basis of agreed procedure. The £1 million worth of proxies disallowed included a considerable number previously pledged to the Committee of Inspection but not properly revoked by individual depositors - as well as a substantial number for which claims had not been properly submitted. This in effect meant that the Committee of Inspection had a majority of 500,000.

Including a proxy by Bryan Fryer-Kelsey alleging he was a £600,000 investor. His name did not appear on the original list of creditors for IIL. James Galliano later told myself and my solicitor Oliver O'Sullivan, that Fryer-Kelsey was added to that creditors' list after he swore an affidavit claiming he was himself an investor.

The meeting, with its obvious attempts at swinging the voting by what I would call a cynical use of the rule-book, proved stormy. Budhrani stood up, pointed out all the irregularities, declared the meeting void, and left. The following Friday the Rock's High Court ruled - in chambers, after two adjournments - that the irregularities were not sufficiently serious to invalidate the creditors' meeting. An official pointer to shady practises? Maybe, but the Committee's victory would stand.

That night we met in the Caleta Place Hotel. Budhrani chaired the meeting, and the 23 investors who'd accompanied us to the island came along. Contrary to the rumours being spread, I'd no wish to hide anything from the people I was representing. Besides, now they were angry, and were taking the action into their own hands.

Gordon Hamill, who'd always been one of my staunchest supporters, told me he was calling an investors' meeting for February, to be held this time in Lurgan. We might have lost the battle, but there were other conflicts ahead. We still had the court action aimed at removing Galliano to prepare for.

Sometimes I act on impulse. It's not necessarily a bad thing, and it's one of the few advantages a private individual like myself has over those who are constricted (in theory, at least) to following the strict dictates of the legal world. The next morning, while the investors bussed across the border into Spain to sample a little of the good life on the Costa del Sol (I mentioned to them that Finbarr Ross still owned an apartment there), I decided to make the acquaintance of Jimmy Galliano.

It wasn't such a rash move. After all, Sam Stubbs had spoken highly of him in one respect at least; he was, above all else, a "gentleman". I reckoned Galliano must feel himself to be under siege, and although I was definitely part of that siege, he'd realise that I was only doing my job.

I took some support with me, bearing in mind that if the meeting developed into a slanging match it would be handy to have a reliable witness around. I chose John Fleck for the job. John, whose mother had invested in IIL, was an investment broker, but entirely unconnected with the cartel. He'd introduced a number of people to the dubious joys of investing the Finbarr Ross way, but realising his mistake, he'd reimbursed them all. John was one of the few good guys in a bad business.

I decided on a non-combative approach, and steeled myself to act in a relaxed and friendly manner. It paid off; Galliano came across.

The meeting was a revelation. I gained the distinct impression that Galliano was an honest man and had been doing his best. But his best just wasn't good enough to hold off the power of the Committee of Inspection. He'd had enough, he said. He wanted out. He wouldn't contest the court proceedings. James Galliano would be only too glad to wash his hands of the International Investments fiasco. He showed me letters he'd written to the Attorney General, asking him to accept his resignation as liquidator.

The meeting was going well - we were almost acting as friends. Another place, another time, and we'd probably have been on the same side. It was going smoothly; too smoothly.

There have been times during this investigation where I'd almost swear the Committee of Inspection had attached some kind of homing device to me. How they managed to keep track of my movements I don't know - I'm not an easy guy to follow - but on this occasion they made their move just in time. The door swung open (no knock) and there was Colm Allen, fuming. He turned to the liquidator and subjected him to a spot of that withering courtroom invective a thousand lawyers know and dread. He asked - demanded - that Galliano terminate the conversation there and then. And never, under any circumstances, was he to discuss anything with Billy Flynn.

"Galliano," he fumed, "Don't you know you work for me?" The meeting was over. I made my excuses, as they say, and left. I picked up the letters to the Attorney General which Galliano had offered me and walked to the door. Allen tried to stop me. There was not a chance, he intimated, that I was leaving that room with those letters. His furious stare bored into me. I looked at his eyes and knew I was looking at a man unlikely ever to sign up for the Billy Flynn Fan Club. He hated me.

I guess it was then he must have noticed John Fleck, impartial third party and potential witness, standing in the room. Fleck told him that not only would I leave unhindered, but the letters were going with me. And for once, I had the better of the finest legal mind in the Republic of Ireland.

We adjourned to the bar of the Holiday Inn, conveniently located next door to Galliano's office, to study the letters in greater detail. Galliano had told me that day he was under pressure from various sources to remain as International Investments' liquidator. It was now obvious that one of those sources was the Gibraltar government itself. Our legal action didn't stand a chance.

• • •

With the possible exception of some encouragement from politicians like Noel Dempsey, Roy Beggs and Alan Dukes, 1988 proved to be something of a disaster for the investigation. When I open my files and see the hundreds of letters I wrote during that year - begging, pleading, threatening, cajoling - I realise now how my daily life had been taken over by the IIL liquidation. I was haunted by it. When I slept, I dreamed of success, or suffered nightmares of final, utter failure. In the daytime I wrote, faxed and telephoned anyone I thought might be able to help. When I was not consumed by this obsession, I retreated once more to the bars and pubs, where a few brandies might at least offer temporary release.

I badly needed support and fresh, sustaining hope. I was beginning to think that Colm Allen might be right, that I'd become unhinged. The trouble with investigating a scandal of this scale is that after a few years you start believing you too are part of it. The events are real, a thousand files testify to that. But the complications suck you in and seem to add a veneer of unreality to everything you do and say. It was impossible to find detachment, an objective view. What had begun as an investigation for others had become part of me. I was no longer just the observer, the hired spy; now I was part of the story.

In December 1987 I'd met in Dublin with Paul Browne, a journalist with the Guardian newspaper. The meeting had been set up by Irish journalist Coleman Cassidy, who had already proved an invaluable ally in maintaining a public profile for the International Investments story. I couldn't make Browne out. One moment he seemed full of enthusiasm for the case, then he'd lose interest and tell me he really didn't know whether there was a good story there at all.

Ironically it was Browne who snapped me out of my depression. In the Spring of the following year I was in London, staying in the Irish Club in Belgravia's Eaton Square, waiting for an investors' meeting the next day. It was another interminable night, and sleep proved elusive. I couldn't seem to take my mind away from its cares; I was again in dire financial difficulties, and they all seemed to be for nothing. The IIL affair was dying.

People were losing interest.

In the paranoia that seems always to haunt a lonely night in a foreign city I fell into my deepest crisis yet. As dawn broke my worries took me wandering, away from the empty elegance of Belgravia and into Victoria where, at five in the morning, I found myself the only customer in an unappetising railway station fast food bar. There are few things in life which can knock a despairing man from the depths of his depression. A British Rail cheeseburger certainly isn't one of them.

I drank coffee to try and keep alert for the meeting, now just a few hours away; tepid, tasteless coffee which looked like week-old dishwater. And at seven o'clock, I bought the morning papers.

Paul Browne had done the story. I couldn't believe it at first. Someone was once more taking an interest. The IIL case hadn't died, and I wasn't mad after all. I read it eagerly. I even got a mention myself.

The second colourful character in the story is Mr Billy Flynn, a private investigator, who has spent nearly three years as the depositors' champion and is near bankruptcy himself. He has been described as a Jack Russell barking at the heels of the establishment.

"Mr Flynn believes he is close to getting results, and police forces on both sides of the Irish border are now taking an interest. But he has made enemies in the Irish government and the business and legal communities both north and south by accusing all the authorities concerned of covering up the fraud to avoid public scandal.

A worryingly accurate portrayal of Billy Flynn - complete with looming bankruptcy and a wide array of enemies - but it was still vindication of a sort. Reading on, there was a disturbing reminder of the point we'd reached in the case.

Mr Galliano told the Guardian that he was going to wind up the liquidation because he did not believe there were any assets remaining, and the extra costs of trying to recover assets would outweigh any money returned. The depositors would not receive any money.

Nothing had changed. We were still fighting a rearguard action to stop the whole liquidation just dying. But at the very least Paul Browne's story would serve as a timely public reminder. If Galliano did shut down the liquidation, there would now be people asking why.

We were still trying to get a new liquidator appointed in place of Galliano, but without much success. The problem was twofold; finding someone willing to take on such a formidable job, and then finding the money to pay them. I'd already tried approaching a couple of the investors themselves, but expert advice suggested that what was really needed was a professional, a chartered accountant with liquidation experience, who was entirely unconnected with the case. I thought I'd cracked it when a Cork chartered accountant named Kieran Moylan agreed to take on the task - on one condition.

Moylan's initial enquiries had found the liquidation to be in total chaos. To get it back on the road, he estimated he would need to bring about 20 legal actions at a cost of around £500,000; he understandably said he wouldn't take the position unless that money was made available by the Government of Gibraltar. Despite a year of intense pressure from the political arena, Gibraltar finally said no to the funding. Goodbye Kieran Moylan.

Then, in 1990, it seemed I'd finally found my man.

John Ross was a partner in a Belfast accountancy firm. He agreed to take over the liquidation (if we could successfully coerce the Committee of Inspection to grant Galliano's most heartfelt wish and let him retire from the case). He seemed enthusiastic, too. He studied all the documentation - no small task - and told us he believed £8 million could be recovered from legal actions against S.K.C., Declan Collins, Colm Allen and Oliver Conlon, Solicitor. But he'd need money to do it. A great many expensive lawsuits were involved. Ross, like Moylan, reckoned it would take half a million pounds to part his (unrelated) namesake from the IIL money.

We decided to approach the International Fund for Ireland, to see if they would fund a new liquidation. Our argument for the Fund's involvement was that the International Investments affair was causing division and distrust between the north and the Republic, exactly what the Fund was set up to combat. We enlisted the help of politicians to apply for funding, to show we were entirely above board. Alan Dukes, Noel Dempsey and Roy Beggs agreed to make the application. Roy Beggs also put a Commons question to the British Industry Secretary, asking if Westminster would cooperate with the Dail to fund lawsuits against the IIL culprits.

But our hopes were dashed. The Fund refused to pay for a new liquidation, claiming the operation simply wasn't in line with their objectives. We now had to attempt the impossible; finding an experienced chartered accountant who would be prepared to fund the operation himself, trusting to the ultimate success of the inevitable lawsuits. Once again the liquidation was becalmed.

• • •

And then something happened. On Friday 16 November 1990, Frank Murray was arrested and accused of conspiracy. A warrant had also been issued for the arrest of George Finbarr Ross.

Murray was arrested in London. The actual charge sheet accused him of conspiring with Ross and others - I couldn't help wondering who these "others" would turn out to be - to defraud International Investments' depositors. The warrant had been issued by the RUC, and Murray was taken to appear in Belfast Magistrates Court. He gave his address - Harrow-on-the-Hill in Middlesex, a posh suburb in London's stockbroker belt - and was remanded on £70,000 bail.

The Sunday Business Post picked up on that word 'others', too, and speculated: "Further arrests may follow shortly in the International Investments affair."

I imagine it will come as no great surprise to you to learn there were no further arrests. The charges against Murray would eventually be dismissed, and the RUC warrant for Ross's arrest was never served. It's still current, and if someone up there at RUC headquarters has lost Ross's Dallas address, I'll be only too glad to refresh their memory.

• • •

David Mairs died in 1991. Our relationship had begun as that of client and investigator, but over the past few years we'd become firm friends. David, you may recall, was disabled; a retired architect who'd invested his savings with Ross to provide the wherewithal for his retirement dreams. David and Emily Mairs had become close friends of my family, too; we'd spent several days with the couple at Glenarm on the Antrim coast.

If my home in County Meath came to be seen as the unofficial headquarters for the International Investments depositors in the Republic, David's cottage served the same purpose for investors in the North. In a sense, David was a colleague.

I visited David a few months before he died in February 1991. We talked and he asked me to promise him something. There was nothing dramatic about it; although he knew he was dying, David wasn't asking me to make a death-bed pledge. He was simply wanting me to carry on, not to crack. Of course, I promised.

I'm not going to tug on your heartstrings with ridiculous accusations that Finbarr Ross and his IIL friends were responsible for the death of a good friend. They weren't; David was dying anyway.

But for one crime I can never forgive them. There might be nothing on the statute books to outlaw the callous cynicism I've met on this case. Ross and his cohorts possess it in abundance. What sort of morality is it when, for the sake of money, you are prepared to rob a man of his dreams?

Chapter Nine

EXPOSURE

In the early years of Gibgate I assumed journalists would hungrily devour information on a scandal of this proportion. It was a complex story, I knew, but one with all the ingredients of good copy. The systematic swindling of the helpless; an identifiable villain living the good life on his ill-gotten proceeds; cover-up on a grand scale. Above all, it reeked of the cynicism of authority - always classic material for a front page.

Gibgate is no less than a national disgrace. And yet, with a few honourable exceptions, the Press has largely ignored it. When Paul Browne's story appeared in the Guardian, I wondered why the British media should seem to be taking a greater interest in the affairs of a Dublin bank than our domestic newspapers and broadcasters. I didn't believe for a moment that Dublin's journalists were in cahoots with Ross or the cartel, but there must have been some reason.

I still don't know for certain. It may have been just a natural reluctance to come to grips with the complexities of the story. Part of the reason I'm writing this book is to try and whip up interest, and if it helps the newspapers to understand exactly what happened with IIL, that will be all to the good. In a democratic society we rely on the media to inform the public, and they in their turn to set up the chain of cause and effect which eventually gets something done in parliament. It's a slow process, but seems to be the only one that works. In the case of Gibgate, I'm hoping this book will prove the catalyst that kick-starts that whole process.

Even I can't really find it in myself to point an accusing finger at the journalists and say: "You did nothing; you allowed this to happen." Honesty forces me to admit that the sight of a rapidly approaching Billy Flynn, files flying in all directions and an obsessive gleam in his eyes, must have frightened off many a hardened hack. Gibgate was so intricate a story that sometimes I was baffled by it myself. The uninitiated journalist, trained to view everything with a cynical eye, must have been floundering.

There was a problem, too, with the journalistic perception of what makes a good story. There were villains - some could even be named in the papers without fear of the usual heavy retribution in the libel courts - but where were the victims? I would point to 1,200 investors, realising as I did so that the game was lost. Investors? The reporter's mind conjured up pictures of wealthy tycoons dabbling in the stock market. No amount of argument was likely to shift that view.

There's a "Catch 22" which operates in Irish scandal stories (of which we've had a few too many in recent years). The journalists want the story easily packaged; they would all like to be Woodward or Bernstein on the trail of the erring President, but few have the time or editorial support for the back-breaking work involved. Too much like being a private investigator, with hardly anything creative involved. Too much leg-work.

So they wait for the story be "authenticated" by someone else. Maybe it'll turn up on the wire services or, more likely, they'll get a call from a political press office. Some politician has latched on to it and wants to use the scandal as a stick to beat his opponents with. (Of course, for that to happen the story already has to have had some publicity - hence the "Catch".)

There were other turn-offs, too. Not only were the victims seen as relatively wealthy investors, but most of them were from the North. The main characters in the story were public figures, but not the easily recognisable villains the journalists were used to (although I'm hoping a few of them get a rather higher public profile when this book is published). There was also the understandable fear of the libel laws, and the possible dire consequences of attacking the sort of people who would be well equipped to defend themselves. Last but by no means least: there was no sex involved. That was fifty percent of media interest ruled out at a stroke.

Yet Ireland's media has done excellent work investigating and reporting many of the country's recent scandals, like Telecom Eireann and Greencore. Perhaps the political element in these stories was more explicit, more obvious.

If newspapers gave the story scant attention, the broadcast media virtually turned a blind eye. Our national broadcasting organisation seems not to have mentioned the story even once. The British Channel 4 consumer programme "4 What It's Worth" devoted a short film to the affairs of Ross and the brokers some years ago, but since then there has been nothing.

Journalists in this late 20th Century are busy people. They have a duty to justify themselves and their actions to superiors. Gone are the days of swanning around the world on a whim and an expense account. I imagine any news editor worth his or her salt would at least raise a critical eyebrow at the sort of costs a reporter would incur while doing a decent job on the Gibgate story.

For whatever reasons, I had my work cut out persuading journalists to cover the story. The more I cajoled them, the more I began to resemble the persona my opponents had invented for me; the obsessive madman touting around his very own conspiracy theory. A few took me seriously; fewer still published the results of their questioning, but to them I am truly grateful. Without their efforts Gibgate would have died, its scandals slipping quietly from public view.

• • •

I knew Elio Malocco well. For a few years I'd worked for the Dublin solicitor as an investigator on a variety of cases. Malocco was retained by the Irish Press newspaper group to defend their libel actions; I'd checked out the background of 30 of those lawsuits myself. We would discuss business and politics over morning coffee near his office. He expressed himself well; he seemed a respectable and plausible man. But for once my intuitions deserted me. Elio Malocco was an embezzler.

Coleman Cassidy also worked for the Irish Press group. Coleman was a journalist, and we met because of Gibgate. In 1986, when the Irish Fraud Squad blatantly refused to investigate International Investments any further, I felt that only media exposure would force their hand. I knew nothing of the workings of the Press, and took advice. Someone recommended I give Padraig Yates a call at the Irish Times. (Journalists, my cynical advisor informed me, would respond far better to a phone call than a letter. Mail slid too easily from desk to wastepaper basket ...)

Yates seemed sympathetic, but he was in the process of writing a book at the time, and felt he could not spare the necessary commitment in time and effort to do justice to the Gibgate story. He gave me another name; Coleman Cassidy of the Sunday Press.

To be honest, Cassidy and I didn't really hit it off at first. He arrived at my office and interviewed me for four hours. When it comes to a grilling, I'm more used to dishing it out than taking it on the chin. He kept demanding evidence. "Prove this; prove that!" I admit I was floundering; I hadn't prepared my case like a barrister in a court of law. I found Cassidy aggressive, and decided I didn't like the man.

I little realised I'd been put through the grilling for my own good. When the questioning was over, Cassidy apologised for his tough approach, but explained it had been necessary to expose any weakness, flaw or inconsistency in my story. He professed himself satisfied with my replies. I had passed the test. He would take on the story. Now I knew what my own clients must feel when they got the third-degree from me.

Cassidy conducted the investigation with typical thoroughness. He talked at length to my solicitors, Oliver O Sullivan in Castlepollard and Stewart Hunter in London, both of whom had worked tirelessly on my behalf, often unpaid, since the start of the case. He contacted Sam Stubbs in Houston and conducted a long interview with him. That interview - you'll already have read part of Cassidy's transcript in Chapter 6 - proved crucial. Michael Keane, deputy editor of the Sunday Press, met with Cassidy and Vincent Jennings on Thursday October 23, 1986. Press day was looming for the Sunday edition, and Cassidy told the meeting he wished to write a story for inclusion that week. They all believed the content of the interview was sensational, and Cassidy made sure Stubbs read and signed his transcription notes as evidence before any story was published.

On Sunday, October 26, the story appeared.

COURT ACTION OVER COLLAPSE OF COMPANY

Negligence claims have been lodged in the High Court against a number of top lawyers and accountancy practices by Mr William Flynn, a financial investigator ... Documents lodged in the High Court cite barrister Colm Allen, acting for the liquidator of ... International Investments Ltd, and his Committee of Inspection, the firm of Stokes

Kennedy Crowley, and two firms of solicitors, Cawley Sheerin Wynne and Barry Edge Manning as defendants in separate plenary summonses.

All are being sued for 'damages and personal loss resulting from the (defendant's) negligence, gross misconduct and fraudulent activity in the affairs of International Investments.'

Coleman Cassidy then went on to explain the background to those claims. It was a story which was to prove costly to the Irish Press group.

The report, to my mind, was a fair and accurate portrayal of the first few months of the liquidation after the removal of Tim Revill. Cassidy had even spoken to Paul Smithwick. Remember him, the leading fund-raiser for the fledgling Progressive Democrats, and director of IIL front company Shelmar? Smithwick pleaded innocence, telling the Sunday Press he was not aware of the ultimate ownership of the company that he had registered. He had no idea it was International Investments. The share transfer had never been completed by Finbarr Ross. The fact that his name had remained in the company's file in Companies Office was an oversight, he said, since he had no dealings with the company since 1984.

Coleman Cassidy was to prove a useful ally in the IIL investigation. He followed the case through its myriad twists and turns, reporting, at intervals, about the attempts to gag Sam Stubbs from giving evidence in Gibraltar, and official investigations into some of the brokers on the cartel. But it was that first story, published on 26 August 1986, which caused the greatest trouble.

The lawyers stepped in. Colm Allen and Declan Collins were claiming the story was defamatory. The main argument was over Cassidy's allegation that Colm Allen, and not Jimmy Galliano, had employed Declan Collins on the liquidation. Cassidy had written:

Mr Colm Allen became the agent in Ireland of the new liquidator and chairman of a Committee of Inspection, representing depositors' interests. One of his first acts was to employ Mr Declan Collins, a partner in SKC to do the liquidation work in Ireland.

That statement was, of course, essentially the truth. While it was certainly correct that Collins was appointed by Galliano, it was on Allen's recommendation. Galliano knew nothing of the man and, therefore, could hardly have made the choice alone. This was later confirmed, when another journalist, Mark Smith from the Sunday Independent, arrived in Gibraltar in September 1991 he asked Galliano about Declan Collins. Smith later reported:

Following his appointment Mr Galliano, on the recommendation of Colm Allen, appointed Dublin chartered accountant Declan Collins - a senior partner with Stokes Kennedy Crowley - as his Irish agent ...

To claim that Cassidy's portrayal of what had happened was inaccurate was, I think, splitting hairs, and unfair to the spirit of the article. I quote from the transcript of Smith's conversation with Galliano.

SMITH : Why did you appoint Declan Collins as your Dublin agent?

GALLIANO : A recommendation by Colm Allen. I knew nothing about Declan Collins at the time, although I knew SKC was a reputable firm. I had no direct contact with Dublin.

Colm Allen also denied ever stating there were no assets in America, as Coleman Cassidy reported he had. I was not present at that interview, and cannot pass comment on what was actually said. We have no option but to trust the outcome of the action, and believe Mr Allen. But the disputed statement was certainly a sentiment he was not shy to express elsewhere. In 1986, he had written the following in a report to brokers that I have in my files: **For the purposes of this Report it is sufficient, I think, to note that there are no assets in America and that the Depositors will recover no money from there.**

• • •

Malocco, incidentally, was a man I knew well, having worked for him on several investigations for cases involving libel actions against the Irish Press group. I suppose we almost became friends. Malocco and I would chat over the news of the day each morning, discussing Ireland's seemingly inexhaustible supply of scams and scandals (perhaps the government should appoint a Minister for them ...)

Working for Malocco helped to pay the bills while I pursued the International Investments case. For a private investigator the work was unusually interesting, too. Flying around the world to work on libel cases certainly beats spending days sitting in a car in County Donegal waiting to serve a writ on a belligerent farmer.

You will probably already know that Malocco turned out to nothing more than a thief; a brilliant lawyer who used his skills and knowledge to cheat his own employer. Malocco embezzled hundreds of thousands of pounds from the Irish Press group during the years he worked for them. By the time that became clear, and Malocco fled the country, I had already changed my mind and grown strongly suspicious of him. My doubts about Malocco's morality began after a incident of an entirely different nature.

• • •

It was way past midnight. I was playing snooker with a close friend at my home. The telephone rang, and the voice on the other end of the line was Malocco. Strange. He rarely telephoned me outside office hours. We were colleagues, and friendly at work, but nothing more. Malocco seemed distressed and agitated. What he was saying was making no sense. Elio Malocco was quaking in abject terror. Someone had put the frighteners on this most brilliant Dublin solicitor. His life was in danger, he said. I was to meet him in the car park of Lamb Doyles, a pub in Kiltiernan, where I would receive further instructions. If I had one, he added, I should bring a gun. (I should perhaps add that, of course, I didn't ...)

It was an irresistible mystery. What on earth could Malocco have been doing which led him to fear for his life? Fingers in the till? Terrorist links?

I thought both these options highly unlikely. The truth proved to be stranger still.

Malocco normally drove a flashy Mercedes, but he arrived at our moonlit rendezvous in the relative anonymity of a Volkswagen Golf. He was taking this seriously. He dashed from the car and ran over to me. Then his story gushed out. Malocco was in love. He had fallen for another woman (he was himself married to Jane De Valera) and her husband was threatening him. It was ludicrous. I pointed out my disgust at his behaviour, but he was moonstruck, his eyes blinded by passion. By passion, and by fear.

The woman's husband had already contacted Malocco, and our noble lawyer now believed a contract was out on his life. It's all a misunderstanding, he told me. Get this threat stopped, he pleaded.

But Malocco, even in the throes of this personal crisis, still retained a little of his lawyer's cuteness. There was something else he wanted me to do. He asked me to help his mistress to sue her husband's solicitors. Malocco didn't miss a trick.

The whole thing was ridiculous. Two grown men, standing in the car park of a country pub in the early hours of the morning. One completely dumbstruck by the whole thing (me) and the other switching roles every few seconds between "Love Story" and "Perry Mason". It was too silly for words. Here was a prominent solicitor asking a private detective to issue legal proceedings on his behalf. Malocco knew that I'd helped others sue successfully by staying in the background and preparing the paperwork for others. Now he was asking me to do the same for him. If anyone else had told me a similar story I'd never have believed it. But Elio Malocco, that night, was behaving as a most irrational man.

But a client is a client, and as far as I was concerned, Malocco - at this time - was still precisely that. I telephoned his mistress's husband from my car phone. I explained about the "misunderstanding". I told him to lay off Malocco, that the man was in my protection now. (I never know why people take this sort of claim seriously, but it invariably works ...) Malocco was ecstatic. He couldn't thank me enough. He owed me his life. I just wanted to get away, back home to the real world of sensible people.

I did eventually meet the woman in question, the new love in Elio Malocco's life. They were in the Berkeley Court Hotel, acting for all the world like a couple of honeymooners, holding hands and gazing into each other's eyes. Cupid's arrow had shot down the legal eagle.

• • •

The Irish Press group was eventually forced to make settlement over Coleman Cassidy's article. The Board of Directors took legal advice that they had no other option; proof had not been forthcoming to support Cassidy's allegations on the appointment of Declan Collins to the liquidation.

The outcome of the action against the Irish Press proved to have widespread implications for future newspaper and media coverage of the IIL affair, and in particular the role played by the Committee of Inspection. The subliminal message had wormed its way into the minds of every news editor in the Republic of Ireland; don't touch the International Investments story ... remember the Irish Press.

• • •

Coleman Cassidy ran several more stories about IIL and its liquidation. None of them proved actionable, but the eventual apology which Colm Allen wrung out of the Press proved an effective gag.

I'm pleased to say Allen didn't get it all his own way, though. He had demanded not only an apology from the newspaper, but from Coleman Cassidy personally. Cassidy refused outright. He told his bosses at the Irish Press that if he was forced to apologise, he would take his talents elsewhere. Cassidy handed the story over to Paul Browne of the Guardian. He'd come to the conclusion that the Irish media was, for all practical purposes, barred from covering it.

I read the result of Browne's trip to Dublin on that lonely morning in Victoria station in April, 1988. When I arrived at the investors' meeting that day I saw I wasn't the only person who'd seen it. Frank Kelly had given the paper a mini-circulation boost; he'd bought a hundred copies of that day's Guardian to pass out to the other investors at the meeting.

Seeing your struggles outlined in print lends a certain measure of official approval to an investigation. For the IIL investors the Guardian story worked its magic. Hope was in the air again; Tony Morgan gave a moving speech, pledging the UK investors would fight for justice until the end. There was spontaneous applause. Frank Kelly gave me more good news. The Sunday News in Belfast had taken up the cudgels on behalf of the defrauded depositors, too. There had been an article in the paper on Sunday April 10. About time, I reckoned, considering most of the people Ross conned were from the North.

That year proved fruitful for media interest. Gerry Melling from Thames Television arrived in Dublin to research and film the Channel 4 documentary programme on the IIL affair. It would concentrate particularly on the role the investment brokers played in channelling money into Ross's bank. The programme, "4 What It's Worth", was broadcast on October 18, 1988. It was presented by reporter Susan Osman, and used tough interrogation, and the techniques of confrontational reporting to allow the words and actions of the brokers to speak for themselves. Several refused to comment or answer Osman's questions; Bryan Fryer-Kelsey, then a member of the Committee of Inspection, told Osman she had asked "a silly question", and drove off without further comment.

The Belfast Sunday News continued to report the liquidation. Reporter Paul Connolly had been assigned to the story, and had now taken over, as far as I was concerned, Coleman Cassidy's role as our conduit to the public. Connolly and his girlfriend Clare came to see me in County Meath. I took to him immediately; Connolly was young, but seemed very bright. He had already developed a full grasp of the International Investments affair - no mean task, I knew. Connolly seemed to have genuine sympathy for the pensioners in the north who were tricked out of their savings. At last - a journalist who understood this wasn't just a bunch of "rich investors", carping about being taken for a ride.

Connolly told me he was working on a major article about IIL for the

Sunday News. He suggested I needed more help from the Unionist MPs in the north, and pointed out that favourable publicity in the Belfast press would help enormously.

On May 22, 1988, the results of his investigations were published. The Sunday News devoted its front page and two inside pages to the International Investigations scandal. And Connolly's political hunches proved correct. Two MPs, Ken Maginnis and James Molyneaux, read the paper that day. In 1991, when I needed further political support, they backed me.

In June of that year the paper ran another story, and then, later that month, there was fresh interest from journalists in the Republic itself. Mick Mulcahy of the Sunday Business Post attended an investors' meeting, and reported to readers:

Creditors of International Investments, the Finbarr Ross offshore bank which went bust seven years ago owing more than £7 million, are seeking the appointment of a new liquidator to pursue individuals associated with the bank prior to its collapse.

London accountant Timothy Clunie was in Dublin last week to meet with creditors. Clunie had been nominated by creditors' representative Billy Flynn to replace incumbent liquidator Jimmy Galliano, who had indicated that he wants to quit the case.

The Department of Justice has repeatedly told Flynn that Garda investigations have failed to uncover evidence of wrongdoing which would justify criminal proceedings in this jurisdiction. However, the issue refuses to go away, not least because Unionist MP Roy Beggs has fought tenacious battles on the depositors' behalf.

The Sunday Business Post renewed my acquaintance in July, 1992, when Gail Seekamp decided I was a central player in the story myself. Modesty forbids me from quoting the title of the piece, which again proved worthy of filling the front page.

He paces the room. Clenching a cigarette in nail-bitten fingers he

reels off names, dates and accusations ... He lists allies and foes, the people who backed his eight year campaign and the others who smeared and obstructed him. Billy Flynn, a 47-year-old private detective, has become the champion of 300 investors who lost their savings when International Investments Ltd collapsed.

'Gibgate - the Untold Story', which Flynn hopes to publish, threatens to expose 'dirty tricks at the highest level of Irish government'.

Read on, and I promise you it will. But I am once more ahead of the story, for I have yet to mention the role of journalist Mark Smith, the reporter from the Sunday Independent who finally managed to track down the elusive George Finbarr Ross.

• • •

If Paul Browne's article on IIL for the Guardian had been the catalyst that kept me on the case and convinced me my obsessive involvement was not madness, Mark Smith's work on the story for the Sunday Independent performed the same function for public perception of the scandal. In 1991 his first article appeared. It was the first time since Coleman Cassidy's writing that a newspaper in the Republic itself had given front-page prominence to the Gibgate affair.

I had persistently pestered Independent Newspapers for attention. I imagine the editors were bemused, possibly even irritated, by the never-ending barrage of letters and revelations from Zimmerman and Company. I didn't care. Persistence, I believe, inevitably pays off. After all, newspapers have to get their stories from somewhere, so why shouldn't they get them from me? This time my war of attrition did the trick.

In the summer of 1991 I had a phone call from a Sunday Independent journalist called Mark Smith. The then Assistant Editor Anne Harris had asked him to see what he could find out about International Investments. I imagine she also had additional motivations, like "... and get this man Flynn to stop bothering me ..."

We arranged to meet. Through June and July Smith drove down to my home on several occasions. Each time I sent him away with his "homework", cardboard boxes groaning with the weight of files, affidavits, letters, faxes and reports. If nothing else, I could keep him in reading matter for months.

Smith was an Englishman and relatively new to the Republic, and I confess I had initial doubts about how soon he'd manage to pick up the intricacies of this most complex of Irish scandals. But he was a professional, and methodically worked his way into the story. We seemed to get on, too; there was something about Smith that appealed to me. He was an intellectual, admittedly - back in London he'd even hosted a literary radio programme - but he had a down-to-earth manner. Unlike so many others in his trade, he appeared to care more for the stories than for acting the role of the journalist. The man seemed thoroughly honest, and I instinctively trusted him. (And like me he was also a chain smoker, although he's now kicked the habit - investigating Gibgate probably took more years off his life than the cigarettes ever did.)

We'd meet in my friend Jimmy Boggans' bar "The Thatch", in Rathcore, just a few hundred yards from my home. Mark Smith was impressed by its old-world atmosphere - so different, he said, to the pubs he'd been used to in London. I would launch into my usual tirade of accusations, scattering the briefings with inevitable sidetracks and political discourse. Smith sat patiently, hearing me out, and then he'd cut straight through the waffle and bring me back on course to the most relevant points. The difficulty with working on a case as involved as IIL for years is that you tend to assume everyone else is party to your thoughts and reasoning. Smith seemed to realise this, and questioned me closely until he was completely satisfied the story was clear in his mind, too.

Once I'd briefed him (and probably forced him to move home to accommodate the mountain of documentation I handed over each time we met) he took the story back to the powers-that-be at Independent Newspapers. I dare say they were amazed: the confusing rant they'd been subjected to from Billy Flynn for years turned out to be a damn good story after all. They sanctioned his expenses - words that must bring a flutter of excitement to any journalist - and told him to do what was necessary. At last I'd found an objective reporter with the wherewithal to follow the story.

Mark Smith set about a thorough investigation of Gibgate. He made the usual phone calls, read through the usual files, and then decided he needed to take it further. Smith flew to Gibraltar to interview Jimmy Galliano, believing he'd find out more if he spoke to the IIL liquidator face-to-face. You'll already have read the transcript of that interview elsewhere in this book. What Galliano told Smith confirmed his journalist's opinion that this was a major scandal.

Back in Dublin, he met Declan Collins at his Dalkey home. Their conversation, unfortunately, was "off the record". Collins' resignation from the IIL liquidation, incidentally - and his early retirement from Stokes Kennedy Crowley - were announced soon after that meeting, just before Smith's piece appeared.

LIQUIDATOR TO QUIT IN OFFSHORE £7M CRASH CASE

The liquidator of the formerly Irish-controlled offshore company International Investments has announced he is to submit his resignation. Gibraltar-based chartered accountant James Galliano has been unhappy for some time with his role in a liquidation in which he can make no further progress.

Mr Galliano was appointed as liquidator of the company seven years ago, in circumstances which he now feels created expectations of him that cannot be realised. 'I wish,' he told me, 'I hadn't become involved. There's been a tremendous amount of shadow-boxing at times. There have been allegations about my appointment that have been painful. It's made it very difficult at times to take positive steps.'

In 1987, Mr Galliano submitted his resignation to Gibraltar's Attorney-General; it was turned down. Since IIL's collapse, he has borne the brunt of the investors' frustration over their missing money. He admits to not being happy with his role in the affair; 'I am isolated to a certain extent,' he says, 'from the places where events took place.

The distance makes it difficult.'

While in Gibraltar Smith had also spoken to Tim Revill, who once more explained his belief that the stolen 7 million was still around: "Seven million pounds of depositors' money ripped off", he said simply, "isn't something that just disappears."

Smith attempted to track down the one person who could provide the authorities with the answer to the biggest question of all - what had happened to all that money? He tried to find George Finbarr Ross.

The last telephone number I could trace for Ross in Houston rewarded me with the unobtainable tone. Other sources, who prefer to remain unnamed, have placed him working in the real estate business in Austin, Texas and rather less specifically 'somewhere in Texas'. Outside of the Lone Star State, he has reportedly been sighted in Vienna.

• • •

Mark Smith eventually found his man. That original story in the Sunday Independent, Ireland's largest circulation Sunday newspaper, had a predictably high impact. People were once more taking the investigation (and Billy Flynn) seriously. My letters to politicians now met with an enthusiastic response, in some quarters at least. Those who had half-believed all those smears and rumours that the whole thing was little more than a figment of my imagination, or that I'd conjured it up to make money (what a ludicrous allegation that was) were now forced to admit that, after all, I'd been right. Ross was a villain. He had swindled the investors of IIL. And the hints of a cover-up deserved, at the very least, an exacting analysis.

The story crossed the Atlantic, to an acquaintance of the braggart Ross, who knew only too well of the con-man's whereabouts. Finbarr was a drinking buddy in Dallas. Every night he sat in the bar and subjected the regulars to dull, boastful stories of polo ponies and the trappings of his wealth. Ross was the high-flyer who insisted on telling everybody about his accomplishments. Ross was the local bore on the bar stool, giving a bad name to ex-patriate Irishmen everywhere. And if this saloon lounge lizard had really swindled old people out of £7 million? Well, the newspapers back in Ireland would have to be told where to find him. So Ross's drinking partner called the Independent, and Ross paid the inevitable price of his careless boasting.

Smith flew to Dallas and booked into the Hilltop Hotel, just down the street from the Tipperary Bar where Ross held court. That evening, he met his informant, and together they went to the Tipperary. And there was Ross, in deep (and loud) conversation with two women. Ten minutes later, he left. Smith learnt he'd be back the following night.

"Next day was a Friday," Smith recalls. "I had to find a photographer, to get visual evidence that Ross was alive and well and living in Dallas. It took hours; Friday is Big Match day in Dallas, and everyone was out taking snaps of the baseball or football or whatever it is these people play. Eventually I tracked down a guy named Chris Demers, and arranged to meet him that evening.

"Chris had prepared well. He'd loaded the right sort of film to cope with the dim light of a bar, and was using high-power telephoto lenses. I'd wired myself up with a miniature tape-recorder and hidden microphone. This time there'd be no argument that what was written was the truth."

Smith went into the Tipperary and waited. His informant had told him Ross would be in at nine p.m. - "regular as clockwork, that Finbarr..." - and Smith prepared the ground by asking the barmaid to introduce them. Ross, he told her, was something of a legend back in Dublin, and he'd be intrigued to meet him. "Sure," she replied, "no problem - Finbarr'll talk to anyone." Smith wasn't planning on telling Ross the real reason for the rendezvous.

The Tipperary was dimly lit. At one end of the bar-room a makeshift stage had been prepared for the traditional Irish band which was scheduled to provide the ex-pats with entertainment later that night. But even in the gloomy interior Smith had no difficulty noticing the arrival of George Finbarr Ross. He had a voice like the proverbial foghorn, and employed it with reckless and regular abandon.

"He was delighted to see me," Smith remembers, "thrilled to meet someone from Dublin. I told him I was a scriptwriter - I had to say something - and that triggered off his own life story. He was only too happy to talk about International Investments. Everything they said about him back home was all lies, he said.

"I had to keep reminding myself that this was a man I shouldn't feel any remorse about deceiving, that this was Ross, the guy who swindled pensioners. He was a loud-mouthed prat but we actually got on quite well."

Smith needed to lure Ross out into the open so Chris Demers could get good photographs. It proved easy.

"Ross was telling me about his car, his Corvette, parked outside. He confided in me that it was great for pulling the girls. I said I'd love to see a Corvette, that I'd never seen one before, and that was all it took. Ross was outside, proudly showing me his Corvette, getting me to sit inside and rev up the engine. And all the time Chris was taking photos of him from a van across the street."

A business colleague of Ross wrote to the Sunday Independent a few days after the story was published. How could they, he complained, besmirch the reputation of his good friend Mr Ross? How could they make up an interview, an interview which never happened, to blacken the name of this respectable Texas entrepreneur? I imagine this man actually believed what he was writing; Ross was still working his magical deceptions.

But this time there could be no doubt. Even on those noisy bar- room recordings which Smith made, there's no mistaking the boastful trumpetings of George Finbarr Ross.

Chapter Ten

THE REFUGE OF SCOUNDRELS

From the start of the International Investments case I knew I needed allies in the corridors of power. The extent of the scandal and its potential repercussions were so great that the backing of those who make the Dail their second home was crucial - otherwise who'd believe a word I was saying?

If I'd taken out a classified advert, it would have read something like **Private investigator with evidence of major cover-up requires support in high places. Applications from Kildare Street particularly welcome.**

Unfortunately, it wasn't that easy. You could say I needed them more than they needed me - so I had to do the looking. The result is that since 1984, my correspondence files have bulged with letters to and from TDs and MPs, and I now have numerous friends at Leinster House, Stormont and the British House of Commons. In the years since the collapse of IIL, politicians have in turn bolstered me up, let me down, praised me, abused me, helped and obstructed me.

But none have ignored me. Even those who, officially, have had "no comment" to make.

• • •

Politics is said to be the last refuge of the scoundrel, but many proud scoundrels I've run across over the years have found this deeply hurtful. Call us rogues if you like, they say, call us cheats, rascals or crooks - but **please** don't mention us in the same breath as politicians.

Now I like to think I'm a fair man, and I find that kind of sweeping condemnation of our administrators a bit harsh. Not all of them are bad - but unfortunately those who are more than overshadow their decent, upright associates. A bent politician equals news, whereas his honest colleague in the constituency next door doesn't. A headline like **MINISTER SEEN NOT TAKING BRIBE** wouldn't sell many newspapers.

But we have a strange attitude in Ireland towards the people we elect to represent us. You could say it was schizophrenic. We expect our TDs to champion our causes, whatever those causes may be; we expect them to work minor miracles on our behalf, to get things done simply by dropping a well-chosen word into the relevant ear. If a country TD walks into his local pub expecting a quiet drink and a read of the paper, you can bet a week's wages on the fact that he hasn't been in the job for long. Within minutes, whether he likes it or not, he'll be surrounded by constituents eager to unload their problems onto their Dail representative, and they'll expect his full attention. A popular Deputy is one who's a good listener, or appears to be. And one who makes a lot of promises.

It seems we have a great deal of faith in our politicians, but little or no trust. I'm not one to bandy figures around - as the coup against Timothy Revill proved, lists of numbers can be dangerous - but I remember a survey claiming that two out of three people believe politics to be the Number One disreputable profession. And there I was thinking my trade had a bad name!

From the late '60s onwards, the Irish political scene became one great big wriggling can of worms, with a few honourable exceptions. Backhanders, slush-funds, lining pockets, oiling the wheels ... you could use all the euphemisms you want, but they all meant the one thing. Corruption. In the corridors of power, in the boardrooms. Corruption that affected all aspects of our everyday lives. Remember the days when you had to wait years to get a phone installed unless you knew the right palm to grease? Remember the days when beautiful Georgian buildings in Dublin were being knocked down to make way for office-blocks nobody wanted, just so a few property developers and their chums in Kildare Street could line their already bulging pockets?

Then recently we had the '91 summer of scandals. Greencore, Telecom, Carysfort; all involved money belonging to you and me (for that's what "public money" is, although you often wouldn't know it) being secretly used to help the fat cats get fatter. It was only when they started being found out that they stopped abusing our funds.

So Charles J. Haughey, one of the best-loved and, towards the end, least-trusted Taoiseachs in the history of the Irish Republic, took his last bow. Rightly or wrongly, he had come to symbolise everything the people thought was wrong with the system, and he had to go. Not only that, but

Haughey had become immensely unpopular with grassroots Fianna Failers. They'd seen him as a traitor to The Party ever since 1989, when to ensure his own political survival he entered into a coalition with Des O'Malley's Progressive Democrats. Many say it was the scandals that did it, but I believe it was the decision to merge with the PDs that spelt the beginning of the end for Haughey.

But I'll tell you one thing. Whether you loved the man or hated his guts - and in my time, I've done both - Ireland won't see another leader like him.

"Grassroots Fianna Failer". There's a term that's often used with a touch of scorn. It brings to mind a vision of a big old fella in a small Midlands town standing proudly behind the counter of the bar-and-grocer's he inherited from his dad. He is solidly Republican, reads the Bible and the Irish Press, goes to Mass each morning and occasionally gets patriotically drunk on a Saturday night. He believes in Ireland, the Lord and Family Values. And, of course, The Party.

To Dublin's wealthy West Brits, this man is no more than a cartoon, a figure of fun. But while they've been busy avoiding their taxes, sneering at the common man and colonising Kerry, it's been this object of their derision who's kept Ireland going.

I make no apologies for sounding partisan. I grew up among those kind of people and, I'm proud to say, inherited their values. As for the devotion to The Party - despite everything, I remain a Fianna Fail supporter.

Considering my family background, that's not surprising.

Let me tell you how my parents met. Obviously I wasn't around at the time, so I have to take my late father Patrick's account on trust. That isn't difficult - he was an honest man, and I like to think he passed that quality on to me.

My father was the youngest of three brothers. Patrick, Peter and Christopher grew up in Kilcock, County Kildare, at a time when Ireland hadn't long been unshackled from Westminster's chains. They were raised in an atmosphere of Republicanism; all became active in the old IRA, and Peter and Christopher would be interned.

My father left school to work for a grocery and hardware store in

Kilcock. His responsibilities included delivering goods to various estates in North Kildare, and he would combine these duties with monitoring and surveillance missions for the old IRA.

While on one such mission at a Kilcock stud farm, Patrick was caught by a young employee, Elizabeth Glass. Elizabeth was just about to report this young man she had found snooping around the estate, but then ... well, to use a well-worn romantic clich , their eyes met - and Patrick remained unreported.

In those days, "mixed marriages" were still very much frowned upon, and Elizabeth, a native of Ballymoney, County Antrim, was a Protestant. But nothing, as they say, gets in the way of love, and Patrick and Elizabeth were married. They had three children; Patrick junior, Michael and yours truly.

The Flynn family has suffered far more that its fair share of ill-fortune. First, my baby brother Michael was the victim of a tragic accident; then my dear father died before his time, leaving Elizabeth to bring myself and my older brother Patrick up on her own. But in an Irish family, no-one's alone for long; my two uncles stepped in, helped support my mother and taught Patrick and me the ways of the world.

The man who provides me with my most vivid childhood memories was Uncle Christopher, known to all and sundry as Kit. In his day, he had been a sporting hero - with Larry Stanley, he'd helped win the 1919 All-Ireland for Kildare - and was as single-minded politically as he had been on the football field.

Even in a staunch Republican family like ours, the strength of Kit's beliefs stood out. He had never accepted the Treaty, or Britain's sovereignty over Northern Ireland; as far as he was concerned, Ireland was still at war with Britain. He accordingly kept a large cache of arms in a shed near his home.

My brother Patrick, who I'm proud to say is these days a successful businessman, became increasingly concerned about Uncle Kit. In the latter years of his life Kit's eyesight began to go, and Patrick was terrified that he'd seriously injure himself rooting around in his shed. Finally, in 1955, he notified the Irish Army of Kit's arms collection. My uncle's civil war was over.

And that, briefly, was Billy Flynn's political education.

• • •

In August, 1984, I went in search of politicians to espouse my cause - or should I say the cause of the ripped-off investors? The two had already become inseparable.

It was my friend John Noland, a retired banker, who suggested I start stirring the political cauldron. This was after the IIL creditors' meeting at Gibraltar's Catholic Community Centre at which Colm Allen and his friends had effectively taken over the liquidation. "The 'Old Hands' have taken control", said John. "Can't you whip up some political support?" Rarely short of an impressive name to throw into a conversation, I told him I'd already arranged to meet my friend Brian Lenihan, then Deputy Leader of Fianna Fail.

Lenihan and I went back the best part of a decade. We had a lot in common; like me at that time, he was unswervingly loyal to Fianna Fail; like me, he was tireless in his duties. Unlike me, though, he played as hard as he worked. You could say he had a reputation for being the life and soul of the party as well as The Party. Along with Charlie Haughey, Brian Lenihan had represented the new breed of Fianna Failer in the '60s and '70s - ambitious, successful and immensely popular with the voters. Many still believe he's the best President Ireland never had.

I'd arranged to meet my friend in the bar of Buswells Hotel, just across the street from Leinster House. It's been said that more political business is conducted in Buswells than in the Dail itself. A conveniently-situated watering-hole for thirsty TDs, political activists and journalists, it has over the years become the main venue for lobbying between Deputies and their constituents. And it was here, in September 1984, that Brian Lenihan and I first discussed IIL.

I sat him down, bought him a drink and poured out my story. It's fair to say he was astonished; he described the affair as "an audacious swindle". We would meet several times over the next year to discuss the matter, but during that time it seemed nothing was actually getting done.

Finally in November '85, after a lengthy meeting at Buswells, Lenihan told me he would attend the next meeting of IIL's Irish investors, which was due to take place the following February at the Irish Club in London. I told Lenihan how disappointed I and the investors were that, after a year, neither he nor any of his colleagues had even raised the IIL matter in the Dail.

I reminded him I hadn't taken my story to Fine Gael, who were then in Government, but to my own political party - because I believed resolving the IIL case could prove immensely valuable to it. Since the majority of Finbarr Ross's victims were Unionists from the North, if Fianna Fail was able to bring about a happy ending to the affair, political bridges could be built between North and South that would be of immense benefit to the party, to IIL's investors, and to Ireland.

Brian Lenihan agreed wholeheartedly with what I was saying, and vowed once again to attend the investors' meeting in London in February. We parted that night the best of friends. I genuinely thought that, as far as high-profile political support for the investors was concerned, I'd cracked it.

But what was about to happen would start me off on the road to becoming the political cynic I am today. I would learn that, in politics, not even friends can be relied upon when the chips are down, and when up against the fat cats the little man doesn't stand a snowball's chance in hell.

So what happened? To put it simply, I was stood up.

In January, Brian Lenihan confirmed the arrangement we had made two months before at Buswells Hotel; he would, he said, be travelling to London with me on February 8 for the investors' meeting. I went ahead and bought plane tickets for the two of us. On the eve of the meeting, February 7, Lenihan confirmed again he'd be travelling with me the next day. I arranged to pick him up at his home in Castleknock, North Dublin, at 7.20 the next morning.

Just before midnight, my phone rang. Unexpected calls at that time of the night usually mean just one thing; bad news, and this call was no exception. On the line was Lenihan. He was sorry, he said, but he had forgotten about an important constituency meeting he had to attend. I would be meeting the investors in London on my own. Our arrangement was off.

For years, I had no idea what made him suddenly change his mind.

• • •

In the next two years, while I kept myself busy by getting heavily into debt and turning myself into Dublin's Least Popular Man in order to keep the IIL story on fire, Brian Lenihan's political star rose and rose. In March 1987, he was appointed Tanaiste and Foreign Affairs Minister in the new Haughey government. I would have phoned to congratulate him, but to be honest my heart wouldn't have been in it. In fact, I probably would have ended up telling him what I really thought of a man who lets down his friends, and in the kind of language that would have made even me blush. So I decided against making that phone call. I wish I had now.

I had been let down by a friend. On top of that, other pressures were piling up in my life that, two years later, would almost kill me.

• • •

After Lenihan had left me out in the cold in early '86, I made contact with the newly-appointed Justice Minister in the Fine Gael Government, Alan Dukes. Looking back, I realise I was foolish not to have brought the IIL scandal to his attention long before I did. After our first contact, Dukes did more for me in three weeks than Lenihan had in three years. It helped that he had (and still has) a powerful intellect, and was seemingly capable of getting to grips with this most complex of cases, involving countless different laws in many different jurisdictions, almost instantly.

Alan Dukes had been plugging away on my behalf ever since our first contact. After Fine Gael was consigned to opposition in 1987, he kept up his sterling work, contacting Brian Lenihan to suggest that something really should be done by the Irish Government about the conduct of the IIL liquidation and the people who had taken it over.

On March 31, 1988, Lenihan wrote to Dukes. In his letter, he indicated that he had no qualms about the way in which the IIL liquidation had been conducted.

Alan Dukes forwarded this letter to me. To say I was shocked would be an understatement; I was, to use a word that's currently in fashion, gobsmacked. What was Lenihan playing at? He knew the facts better than anyone.

I picked up the phone and dialled my friend's number, as I had so many times over the past ten years - to arrange to meet for a drink, to ask after the family, just to have a chat. But this time it was different. This was no social call - I wanted to know what the hell he thought he was doing.

Lenihan, I would guess, had been expecting such a call. Whoever answered the phone informed me that he didn't wish to speak to me. I tried again; same result. My one-time friend was now refusing to take my calls.

Looking back, I admit my subsequent behaviour was hardly that of a responsible, middle-aged husband and father, but I was deeply hurt. Not only by what Lenihan had done, but by the fact that the IIL case seemed to be back at Square One again, as it had been so many times. It seemed that no matter how hard I worked, no matter how many leads I followed up and how much paperwork I ploughed through in search of evidence, I was right back where I started.

I began to drink heavily. As I've said elsewhere in this book, I've always liked a drink, but have never indulged while on duty and have always been able to take it or leave it. But, as the Japanese say (I think I'm right): "First the man takes a drink, then the drink takes a drink, then the drink takes the man." In the spring of 1988, stung by Brian Lenihan's rejection, making no headway in the case that had virtually taken over my life, the drink took me.

I don't remember much about that April. One day blurred into another. I spent a lot of time just sitting at my desk staring into space, the trusty brandy-bottle at my side, while its empty cousins piled up higher and higher in the corner of my office. I think I would have given up altogether - if it wasn't for Eileen.

I've sung the praises of my wife already, I know, to the highest heavens. I've virtually beatified her. But if you'd lived with Billy Flynn for as long as she has, you'd know she deserved all the praise on this earth, and more. A caring husband and father I know I am, but that isn't always enough. All the good intentions in the world can't compensate for life with a drunken zombie.

One morning late that April, I went to the kitchen for - I forget what for. Maybe another bottle of brandy. It was a bright, sunny morning, the kids had been packed off to school, and all was tranquil on our acre of County Meath. But Eileen was in the kitchen crying - and, like a blind man who's been given a miracle cure, I suddenly saw as clear as day just what I must have looked like to the woman I love.

At that very moment, I'm glad to say that seeing her husband standing there unshaven, pallid and shaking - in short, a wreck of a man - caused the usually tolerant Eileen to snap. She turned on me. She told me in no uncertain terms what I was doing to her and the kids, and she gave me an ultimatum. Either seek treatment for what had become my drinking problem, or our marriage was over.

There's nothing like the prospect of losing everything that's important in your life to sober you up, and I was facing that prospect right there in that kitchen. I phoned our family doctor in nearby Summerhill, and went straight out to see her.

Dr. McEntee took one look at the bloodshot, haggard husk that just a couple of months before had been Billy Flynn, and told me I needed hospital treatment. I explained that, since I was thousands of pounds in debt because of my work on the IIL case, I couldn't afford the specialised treatment she was talking about. Reluctantly, she advised me of a way I could treat myself at home, under the watchful eye of Eileen.

For the next two weeks, I was home and dry - literally. As strength and sobriety returned, reality came with it, and I did what I'd been putting off doing for so long - my accounts. When I'd finished, I knew why I'd been delaying that particular chore I was £347,000 in debt.

I reacted to the pressure of owing so much money to so many people by going through every middle-aged man's nightmare. A few days later, while on a break with Eileen and the kids in Bettystown, I had a heart attack and was rushed to Navan Hospital.

I was lucky; the fellow with the scythe had spared me this time. During my convalescence, I had time to think. Never again, I pledged, would I have anything to do with International Investments. Finbarr Ross, Declan Collins, Colm Allen and the rest of them - I never wanted to hear their names again. I wanted to live, and live as normal a life as possible.

Unfortunately, my friends had other ideas. John Noland, Gordon Hamill and Christy Timmons from the Ulster Bank in Kilcock, among others, visited and told me I should carry on. But this time it wasn't concern for IIL's investors that swung my decision. It was concern for my marriage.

Of the ~347,000 that I owed, £340,000 of it left me relatively unconcerned. When your debts are as massive as that, they cease to be tangible - on paper, they look more like phone numbers than sums of money. It was the remaining £7,000 that had come close to costing me my life. That sum was owed to local people, and I felt certain that if Eileen found out about my debts in our own back yard, so to speak, she'd leave me for sure. So when Gordon Hamill and Christy Timmons raised £7,000 to enable me to pay off those local debts, I felt I owed them something in return. Don't get me wrong - no pressure was put on me to finish the case. They left it up to me. But ... well, they'd done me a favour. And, if I'm honest with myself, the stronger I got the more defiant I became.

I've said I don't like getting beaten. Sitting up in my hospital bed, watching those less fortunate than me being wheeled around the ward by nurses, I reckoned I had put too much time, energy, cash and emotion into the IIL case to just let it go now.

I would carry on. If Eileen would let me.

When I told her what had been going through my mind she raised her eyes to heaven, but vowed to stick with me. As, for reasons known only to herself, she has to this day.

Once again - thank you, Eileen. With all my heart.

•••

I was back on the case, and a politician who had taken an interest in my story for over a year was beginning to make waves. He was my local Fianna Fail TD, a young former schoolteacher named Noel Dempsey who in his previous calling had taught my eldest son Patrick.

I had first got in touch with Dempsey soon after he was elected in March 1987. He agreed that the events surrounding the collapse of IIL seemed a matter for concern, and asked to see my files related to the case. Among my good qualities is not, I am ashamed to say, a respect for trees; I collect paperwork like a squirrel hoards nuts. I photocopy everything in triplicate. I write more letters each week than I can count. Friends of the Earth would hate me.

Anyway, Noel Dempsey had asked to see the files, and see the files he did. I thought I saw his eyes glaze over when I first pointed out the boxes full of affidavits, depositions, letters, balance-sheets and reports that I had accumulated in just three years, but that could have been my imagination. I spared him the ordeal of looking through it all, and handed him instead the condensed version of my work on the case.

On September 7, 1987, Noel Dempsey wrote me the following letter - and in doing so, convinced me I had picked the right name for the affair.

Re: "GIBGATE"

Dear Billy,

Thank you for your letters and enclosures regarding above which I am at present studying.

From my initial reading of the documents you sent to me, it seems that you certainly have the whole affair aptly named.

Perhaps we could make an arrangement to meet and you could let me know how you feel.

Kindest regards,

Yours sincerely,

Noel Dempsey, T. D.

Dempsey has proved to be my most loyal ally in the Dail. At the time of writing (September '92) he is rapidly climbing to the top of the Fianna Fail tree - and quite rightly so - but has never lost interest in the case. At the time he first became involved, he was to find, as I had, that in the case of International Investments it seemed all the laws of the land could be re-written on a whim. The kind of evidence that would, in any other circumstances, be regarded as irrefutable was simply being ignored.

As an example of what I'm talking about, I give you this letter, written to Dempsey on February 29, 1988, by the then Justice Minister, Gerry Collins:

I wish to refer to your representations on behalf of Mr. Billy Flynn, Enfield, Co. Meath, regarding alleged fraud involving International Investments Limited.

I have had enquiries made of the Garda authorities in the matter. They have informed me that their investigation is on-going, but that despite extensive enquiries no evidence has been obtained to warrant a criminal prosecution ...In the circumstances there is no further action that the Gardai can take in relation to criminal proceedings unless evidence which warrants a prosecution comes to light.

What more "evidence that warrants a prosecution" did they want? They already had the boxes and boxes of the stuff I had bombarded them with since 1984. Perhaps it would have taken Finbarr Ross himself to grab the Garda Commissioner by the scruff of the neck and yell in his ear "I CONFESS TO HAVING COMMITTED A £7 MILLION FRAUD ON IRISH SOIL, WHICH CAUSED HUNDREDS OF PENSIONERS TO LOSE EVERYTHING!" to stir the Gardai into taking action.

On second thoughts, they'd probably have dismissed that as insufficient evidence too. Let's face it - Ireland's authorities would rather set fire to Leinster House than prosecute Finbarr Ross or investigate the liquidation of IIL.

Back in 1988, Noel Dempsey was learning fast that if a man like Ross has friends in high places, he is given a free rein to do virtually anything he likes with no fear of investigation or prosecution. On February 26 that year, the following article appeared in The Phoenix magazine:

Noel Dempsey, the young Fianna Fail TD for Co. Meath, got the surprise of his life last week when he was advised at the eleventh hour by the Ceann Comhairle that questions he had down for the Minister for Justice on the Thursday before the Ard Fheis could not be heard.

The ceisteanna were in relation to International Investments Limited, the ill-fated Gibraltar-registered offshore bank set up by Dunmanway's own, Finbarr Ross ...

Was the Government proposing to take action, Dempsey wanted to know, against those who had taken deposits ... Were the Gardai investigating and was any action being taken against the Gibraltar

authorities to retrieve the £5 million lost by Irish depositors?

The matter was sub judice, he was told, as there were a number of High Court hearings pending in relation to IIL ... involving private investigator William Flynn, who has taken up the cudgels on behalf of a substantial number of IIL investors.

Whoever dreamed up the idea of using my fight for justice as a reason for disallowing a Dail question on IIL has a twisted sense of humour that, given different circumstances, I'm sure I could appreciate. But to this day, I fail to understand how Noel Dempsey's straightforward, fact-seeking questions about the case, which would have been asked within the privileged confines of the Dail, could possibly have been sub judice.

Dempsey, as I said, was learning fast. He was, especially, learning that a lot of people had a lot to lose if the truth came out. A few weeks after we first met, the TD wrote a letter to IIL's investors informing them that he was investigating the case. It didn't take long for the alarm to sound. Soon after his letter went out, Dempsey received a "warning-off" letter from Colm Allen and the Committee of Inspection. "They told me the case wasn't worth following up", Dempsey said in a recent interview. "They said Billy Flynn was totally irresponsible and in it for gain."

Then came a phone call from Declan Collins, describing me as "mad and dangerous". Three years later, Dempsey and Collins were to meet. The occasion was Charles Haughey's Presidential Dinner at the Berkeley Court Hotel in Dublin; the date was December 8, 1990. Collins, having been introduced to Dempsey, took the TD to one side. He advised him not to have anything to do with me; he warned that I was a "madman", a "lunatic", and a "dangerous person to be associated with".

"I became suspicious", Noel Dempsey recalled recently, "of the number of people trying to blacken Billy Flynn."

In 1989, despite a senior member of the Garda urging prosecution, the DPP decided there was "insufficient evidence of fraud" to warrant any action. "I think", said Dempsey, "it's a case of 'we wish it would go away'. People are afraid of opening this can of worms. But it certainly appears there has been a massive fraud and no serious efforts made to bring its perpetrators to justice."

•••

Which other politicians have helped out Flynn in his crusade? It's time, I think, to include a short roll of honour here. Aside from Alan Dukes and Noel Dempsey, whose sterling efforts on my behalf you already know about, I have received help and support from, among many others, John Bruton, Ivan Yates, Roger Garland, Liam Lawlor and Jim Fitzsimmons in the South, and James Molyneaux, Ken McGuinness and Roy Beggs in the North. More on the hard work of the last gentleman - who, more than anyone, has been responsible for ensuring the words "International Investments" are currently in common usage at the British House of Commons - can be found in the concluding chapter.

In October 1987, having tried and failed several times to make contact with Charles Haughey, I mailed a comprehensive file on the case to his daughter Eimear, who I knew slightly. I asked Eimear if she could draw the file to her father's attention. A few weeks later, I received the following letter:

Dear Mr. Flynn,

My daughter Eimear has passed me correspondence relating to a case in which you are involved. I appreciate the distress that can be caused to individuals by the collapse of any financial institution, but I regret to have to tell you that I cannot see that there is any way in which I could be of assistance in a matter of this kind.

Yours sincerely,
Taoiseach

The man who was once my political idol - who in 1991 I realised was somewhat less than perfect - was about as much use to me when times were hard as a lifeboat in the desert.

•••

The Fianna Fail of today is not the party to which my family gave its devoted support, nor the party I myself believed in unquestioningly for so many years. It no longer cares for the welfare of the common people - those very people who created it. It is now little more than the political wing of the business community. So perhaps it isn't surprising that, following their electoral triumph in 1987, it was people at the highest levels of the new Fianna Fail Government who took no action over International Investments.

And what of the new force in Irish politics - the party of the "high moral ground"? What has it done to bring the facts of this case out into the open?

I'm talking, of course, about the Progressive Democrats - those half-dozen political itinerants who, at the time of writing, hold the balance of power in the Dail. The party's major selling-point has always been its lily-white image. Its members claim to abhor skeletons in cupboards. So how have the PDs, and their leader Des O'Malley, responded to the IIL scandal?

With a deafening silence; the kind of outright refusal to acknowledge the facts that's worthy of their reluctant partners in coalition, Fianna Fail.

I had first made contact with Des O'Malley when, in 1988, I sent him a copy of Paul Browne's Guardian article about IIL, plus a pile of supporting evidence. A couple of weeks later, I received an acknowledgment that he had received, and was reading, the correspondence. In the same year, the PD TD for Dun Laoghaire, Geraldine Kennedy (who was to lose her seat, as were so many PDs, in the '89 General Election), passed on all my IIL files to the party's high-profile justice spokesman Michael Mc-Dowell. Unlike his boss, McDowell didn't even bother to reply.

In January '89, having heard nothing further from the Progressive Democrats, I delivered a major file on the affair to their headquarters at 25, South Frederick Street in Dublin. This file contained all the up-to-date evidence and documentation any politician wishing to take the matter further would have needed. The response? Silence.

In May 1990, wheelchair-bound IIL investor David Mairs wrote to the then Justice Minister, Gerald Collins. It's fair to say David's letter was desperate. I've lost everything, was its message. Isn't there something - **anything** - the Irish Government can do? Collins forwarded the letter to Des O'Malley, then, as now, the Minister for Industry and Commerce. When David Mairs died in February '91, he was still waiting for O'Malley's reply.

On June 19, 1991, I myself wrote again to O'Malley, suggesting that he should exercise his ministerial duties in the IIL affair. Despite knowing the facts of the case inside out by now, his response of July 2 simply stated that he had no intention of taking any action.

On September 16, I tried one more time to whip up some concern among Ireland's political mould-breakers, writing to the Michael McDowell, now the PDs' chairman, to enquire why his party had done nothing about the scandal. Having heard nothing by October 1, I wrote again - and yet again on October 11.

Now I know Mr. McDowell is a busy man - with a grand total of six Deputies to look after, he must be - but surely that wouldn't stop him briefly acknowledging receipt of my letters? Or perhaps it's easier to simply ignore them.

In October, I received an interesting phone call.

Let me fill you in, briefly, on the background to it. Among the maze of companies subsidiary to International Investments Ltd. was one called Kenansville. In his deposition, sworn in Houston in August 1984, Finbarr Ross said he believed Pat O'Malley was the 25% owner of Kenansville. Pat O'Malley, the cousin of Des O'Malley, went on to become a Progressive Democrats TD; after he lost his seat in the 1989 General Election, he became an adviser to Bobby Molloy, PD TD and Energy Minister in the coalition Government.

So on October 10, 1991, my office phone rang. On the line was John Loughrie, Bobby Molloy's private secretary, and he was worried. Mr. Molloy, he said, has heard rumours about his adviser Pat O'Malley's involvement in IIL and is extremely concerned. Obviously any blot on O'Malley's copybook would mean immediate removal from the post. Could I let Mr. Molloy have a copy of the transcript of Finbarr Ross's deposition?

I said I could, and that I would drop it off at the Department of Energy myself. No need, said Loughrie. We'll send someone to Meath to collect it.

Sure enough, within a couple of hours a man from the Department of Energy arrived to collect the transcript from my office. Don't ask me why, but my suspicions had been aroused, and I had one of my employees tail him back to Dublin.

Unfortunately, somewhere in the labyrinth of one-way streets that passes for central Dublin's road system, my man lost sight of his quarry. Parking his car near the Dail, he walked into Buswells Hotel to phone me with the bad news - and saw something that made his unexpected day-trip more than worthwhile.

While my man was in the lobby looking for change for the phone, Bobby Molloy walked in with Pat O'Malley. My man saw Molloy hand O'Malley a document, which he recognised as the transcript of Ross's deposition collected from my office in Meath just an hour before. The transcript that contains the following lines:

Q : Who owns the other 25 percent (of Kenansville)?

ROSS : I am not quite sure. It may have been a chap by the name of Pat O'Malley.

In fairness to Pat O'Malley, records in the Companies Offices do not indicate that he was a shareholder in Kenansville, as alleged by Finbarr Ross.

•••

To the Progressive Democrats, as to most of Ireland's politicians, lawyers and businesspeople, Billy Flynn spells bad news. He tells them facts they do not wish to know. He obstructs the smooth running of a crooked country. Letters from his pen, when not met with a curt rebuff, are consigned to that round wire pending-tray in the corner of the office known as the waste-paper basket.

"Bin Flynn" could be the Irish Establishment's unwritten creed. Spread the word around that he's a nutter, make threatening calls to his home, ensure his life is made generally unpleasant - and he might just go away.

No such luck, I'm afraid.

Chapter Eleven

GIBGATE

In front of me on my desk is a file. Its cover is a well-thumbed cardboard folder. An adhesive label bearing the title of the file hangs, only half stuck, from the front of the document. The label, now just a grubby strip of plastic, is one of those embossed affairs you knock out in an idle moment of a dull day. Over the years the file has seen heavy use, and the label has curled around itself. Without forcing the label back onto the paper, only part of the title is visible. From where I sit I can just make out the second half of the second word, which reads " ... estors".

Were anyone to make the effort to glue back the tattered label they would find it bore the title "IIL Investors." If that person then went on to open the folder he would find a comprehensive list of the clients who came to me for help in the International Investments affair. A long list.

Their names are indexed down the left hand side of each page. Then there is a space, and typed down the centre of the page is a row of figures. Those numbers are the amounts of money Finbarr Ross stole from each of the investors. Some of the sums do not appear to be the stuff of grand larceny, while others run impressively into six figures.

Next to the file lies a pocket calculator. I've just been using it to work out some numbers of my own. The result is sobering. Not a single person lost as much money in the IIL affair as I did.

• • •

I am tired of International Investments. The investigation, of which I'd had such early hopes, has made me bitter. The full list of what it has cost me cannot be made out in pounds and pence. I can't even begin to itemise the toll of its passage. Perhaps I could mention specifics. The brutal debts I still struggle to pay off; the smears on my character and profession; the allegations of madness; the heart attack; the drinking; the strains on my family which brought us close to the point of breaking. These are mostly finished with now, but they still leave their scars.

You may think me a shirker or a quitter, but I want out of the whole damned affair. There's no longer any possible rational justification for going on. It has been no less than a fight, and I have been bruised and bloodied. And I seem, for the moment, to have lost it.

A few thousand words ago I mentioned a headline in the Sunday Business Post, and told you my modesty forbade me to repeat it here. I have changed my mind. There is something ironic about the assumptions it makes, the neat pigeon-hole to which I appear to have been consigned. The headline says **VICTIMS' HERO BLAMES SYSTEM**. Do they mean me?

Right now, as I stare at that faded file and wonder how on earth I can draw conclusions from such an inconclusive affair, the accolade of "hero" almost sickens me. For what have I done? What results do I have to show for the years I toiled over IIL? What has this "hero" actually won for these victims?

Down the right hand side of every page of that investors' file there is another column, a vertical strip of white paper a couple of inches wide. Back on May 26, 1984, when I began the document, I included it to leave enough room for reporting my expected successes with each individual case. (No-one ever praises a private detective, so you're forced to do it for yourself.)

When anyone tries to call me a "hero", I only have to glance at that column to bring myself back down to earth. It is completely empty.

No, there is no single rational reason for me to continue with the case which almost destroyed me. Perhaps, then, it is fortunate I am sometimes an irrational man.

• • •

It is now September, 1992 - one hundred months since I began to investigate the affairs of International Investments. In many ways, the fight must now be carried on by others. It is the task of my allies in the Dail and the Commons to apply pressure in the directions their expertise tells them it will best be employed. I am not quitting - although I would dearly love to - but my role must now be that of a supporter, rather than a leading protagonist. This book forms a major part of that support.

Gibgate - The Untold Story is now almost finished. Two days ago I went with my solicitor to see our barrister, who had already been sent a copy of the manuscript. I asked him what he thought.

"It's certainly a hell of a story," he told me. That I knew. But was there anything at all actionable in it?

There was a sharp intake of breath. Then he began to chuckle.

"First I'll tell you the good news," he eventually replied. "There's a tiny section in Chapter 7 which I can absolutely guarantee won't get anyone upset ... "

• • •

So what is happening now? What is the state of play, eight-and-a half years since Billy Flynn, private investigator, family man and one-time political idealist, took up the cudgels on behalf of IIL's investors?

Those investors are no nearer to getting their cash back than they were when Timothy Revill, the man who did too much, was removed as liquidator in August 1984. As I've said elsewhere in this book, most have given up hope of seeing their money again - and who can blame them? The word from Dallas is that Finbarr Ross has now started to actually do a bit of work for a living. Who knows how much of the £7 million he misappropriated is left?

I know one thing. Ross has been living high on the hog in Texas, squandering the hard-earned cash of those he ripped off on the soulless, materialistic lifestyle that is so dear to him. A fast woman here, a flashy car there, a dud property deal there (for Finbarr Ross never did have a head for business. Like most of society's parasites, his only real talent is for the swindle, the stroke, the fast one). Not only has this con-man managed to escape justice, but to escape it in comfort. The kind of comfort you or I could only dream about.

One thing you can say for sure about any sum of money is that it won't last forever. Even £7 million. As each day of Irish Government inaction passes, a little more of the IIL investors' cash is being frittered away by

Finbarr Ross. On a meal for two at one of Dallas's $150-a-head restaurants; on this month's rent for the premises of his latest "investment banking" business; on a tankful of gas for his Corvette. And maybe on another pair of Italian leather shoes.

Eventually, Ross will spend it all. If no official action has been taken by then, will that be the end of the story? Will Billy Flynn admit defeat, file his crusade under "Unfinished Cases" and retire meekly to the green fields of Meath?

Not on your life.

• • •

Press statement from the office of Roy Beggs, Ulster Unionist MP for East Antrim, released August 8, 1992:

Petty thieves and shoplifters are being prosecuted every week. It is about time that the crooks associated with International Investments were brought to justice.

A constituent of Roy Beggs MP ... invested over £20,000 of his savings between 1982 and 1984. He continued to ask for audited accounts but never received them ...

The Secretary of the Committee of Inspection and the solicitor appointed by them in Gibraltar have never replied to correspondence even when stamped addressed envelopes were enclosed.

Which, of course, should surprise no-one.

In the last five years, Roy Beggs has become perhaps my greatest ally in the whole saga of IIL. The MP for East Antrim became involved after a call in 1987 from a constituent, who'd been robbed of everything by Finbarr Ross, and wanted to see something done about it. His name was David Mairs.

Beggs and I first made contact in early '88. Since then, he has devoted much of his precious time and energy to bringing the scandal to the attention of the British House of Commons. If this case has taught me one thing, it is that you should never judge a man by his political persuasion; if you'd told me ten years ago that I'd be working with an Ulster Unionist, I would have said you were as mad as certain people have claimed I am.

But, these days, the cries of "lunatic" seem to have abated. Perhaps it's a result of the changing tide of Irish opinion regarding the accountability of those in positions of power and influence; but no-one is calling me mad now.

• • •

From the Cork Examiner, August 6, 1992.

Industry and Commerce Minister Des O'Malley is now under increasing pressure to order an inquiry into the collapse of International Investments Ltd. Mr. William Flynn, a legal and financial investigator from Enfield, Co. Meath ... said that a number of deputies, among them Alan Dukes and former Minister Micheal O'Kennedy, had undertaken to table questions in the Dail. Former Foreign Minister Brian Lenihan had indicated support for a judicial inquiry ...

Unionist MP Roy Beggs has tabled a question to Foreign Secretary Douglas Hurd asking if Britain, which is the governing power in Gibraltar, can do anything to help the investors who lost money in the crash. This is due for answer when Parliament returns in October.

On July 2, 1992, I travelled to London for a meeting with Roy Beggs at the House of Commons, to introduce him to Tim Clunie, the liquidator I hoped would be appointed. As we passed through the security screen, I reflected on the irony of the situation - here I was, the offspring of one of Ireland's staunchest Republican families, about to sit down to lunch with a

Unionist in the Parliamentary heart of the old British Empire.

After lunch we retired to a lounge overlooking the River Thames for some serious discussion of the IIL case. Roy Beggs told me the one thing he wanted, which the Irish Government had withheld from him, was the IIL liquidator's report. I replied that the authorities would never make it available.

Beggs suggested otherwise. He told me he would be going directly to the Taoiseach himself. "This is a cover-up by the Irish Government", he alleged. "You will have my total support in exposing it." He rose, saying he would be back in 15 minutes.

On returning, he handed me a letter. "I have just faxed this", he announced, "to Albert Reynolds."

Dear Prime Minister Reynolds,

Many of my constituents in East Antrim have lost their entire life savings as a result of the International Investments Ltd. Gibraltar scandal.

Why has the Government of the Irish Republic so far failed to appoint a High Court inspector to investigate the case?

Will you seek to obtain justice for my constituents, and at the same time dispel the widely-held perception that there has been a cover- up at high level within the Irish Republic?

In the ten weeks since that fax was sent on July 2, 30 TDs and MPs made similar representations to Albert Reynolds. Reynolds, quite correctly, passed them on to his Minister for Industry and Commerce, Des O'Malley. Over 70 politicians have now pledged support for IIL's investors in one way or another.

The Taoiseach has been under constant pressure from Noel Dempsey and 10 other Fianna Fail TDs to order O'Malley to take action over the

IIL collapse. These deputies feel, as I do, that a High Court inspector should be appointed to investigate the scandal. So strong is the level of political support for this initiative that, if O'Malley fails to take it, a motion of no confidence in him looks increasingly likely.

On September 17, 1992 - the day before the printer's deadline for this book - Des O'Malley's private secretary, Patrick Kelly, told me his boss is standing firm. No High Court inspector will be appointed to look into IIL if Mr. O'Malley has anything to do with it. "There will be no change", said Kelly, "in the Minister's position on this matter." And the Minister's position? Do nothing. Mr. O'Malley has also failed to take any action over questions arising from the sale of four acres of government land in Dundrum - known as the Somerville property - to South Frederick Holdings. Finbarr Ross claimed in his Houston deposition that IIL owned a 20 percent share in that company.

From a letter to Liam Lawlor TD from Des O'Malley, July 31, 1992.

While I have certain powers under the Companies Act relating to the appointment of Inspectors to conduct investigations into the affairs of companies, I consider that, in view of the length of time since (IIL) was operative, the inevitable difficulties that arise in investigating foreign incorporated companies and the fact that the matter has already been investigated by the Gardai in the context of previous allegations, no useful purpose would be served by invoking the powers in question.

Do nothing. Just hope it goes away.

• • •

Letter from Brian Lenihan to the author, July 28, 1992.

Dear Billy,

I have made contact with the Taoiseach and pointed out the importance of appointing an Inspector under the Companies Act to investigate the affairs of International Investments Ltd. and their subsidiaries and associates.

Best wishes.

Brian Lenihan and I, I'm glad to say, are friends again.

A month before that letter was written, at Buswells Hotel (where else?) we met for the first time since the events of 1987. Brian told me he had been misled about the IIL liquidation; he had been misinformed within his own department, and wanted to apologise.

He didn't have to. I had carried out my own investigations, and knew the identity of the person in the Department of Foreign Affairs who had sidetracked Brian Lenihan back in '87. Ireland's best-loved politician, as far as I'm concerned, is completely exonerated.

• • •

So who is standing in the way of Billy Flynn, and by extension in the way of victory for IIL's investors, now?

You could say Des O'Malley and the Government of Gibraltar are obstructing us by default. Both have different reasons for not wanting anything done; both have the power to make things difficult purely through lack of action.

Declan Collins? He's out of the picture now, and has been since his early retirement from Stokes Kennedy Crowley in 1991.

And Colm Allen?

Member of the Bar Council.
Member of the Library Committee of the Bar Council.
Member of the Standing Committee of the Bar Council.
Member of the Public Affairs Committee of the Bar Council.
Member of the Solicitors' Liaison Committee of the Bar Council.
Member of the Council of King's Inns.

Member of the Irish Bar.
Member of the English Bar.

Colm Allen remains the Chairman of the Committee of Inspection of International Investments Limited (In Liquidation).

• • •

From my last report to IIL investors (Report No. 42) - September 3, 1992.

I wish to take this opportunity of informing investors that I have brought an application before the Supreme Court of Gibraltar for the appointment of joint liquidators T.A. Clunie of S.G. Bannister & Co., London, and John Bassett, a member of the Gibraltar Financial Commission. This application is being opposed by John Barbour, Colm Allen and James Galliano who wish to terminate the liquidation and would prefer you forget about IIL and those who robbed you.

I have done my very best for you over the past 8 years, but all my relentless efforts were meaningless because of the Irish Government cover-up. However, on the plus side, you will be pleased to be informed that over 70 politicians have now pledged support for the investors, as will be disclosed in the Press in the near future. With this political support in mind, my Irish and London solicitors will travel with me to Gibraltar on Thursday the 1st of October, when we will make a demand for a full refund of investment, plus interest, on behalf of all the depositors.

I want to assure you that I will not rest until I have brought to justice all the individuals who robbed you and those who assisted them in covering up the affair.

Yours sincerely,

William Flynn

• • •

Ireland is a troubled country. Parts of our land are, quite literally, still at war. Broadcast your patriotism abroad and you know only too well the reaction you get, the international perceptions of this divided island. The tragedies and outrages will come tumbling out. Bloody Sunday. Enniskillen. The hunger strikes. Every Irish man or woman knows how the world perceives us, and it is a profoundly saddening burden we are forced to bear.

Ironically, it is the corrupt shambles of Gibgate which has given me my brightest hope for how things could be, a glimpse of a better future for both north and south. On Monday, January 25, 1988, for one evening, the frontiers were forgotten.

I was drinking with Coleman Cassidy in the Caleta Palace Hotel in Gibraltar, where we'd decided to hold an investors' meeting. We were a sombre crowd that night; investors, lawyers, a journalist and a private eye. With one thing in common. We'd lost a battle.

Cassidy and I were standing on the balcony outside the lounge. The Caleta Palace has a unique geographical distinction; it's the most southerly hotel in Europe. Across the black waters of the Straits of Gibraltar we could just make out the lights of Ceuta. Cassidy turned to me and pointed something out. Here we all were, far from our homes. We were Unionists from the north, Republicans from the south. Catholics and Protestants. The rivalries of history and politics were forgotten. We were Irish. And we certainly weren't going to surrender without a fight.

Even tragedy sometimes teaches valuable lessons. The wall that divided us was a barricade of our own making. Whatever the practical obstacles in our way, here was positive proof that we shared common ground. A continent away from our world of bullies, bluster, barbed wire and bullets, there was nothing to tell us apart.

There is an adversary at work in Ireland more powerful than our centuries-old partisan duel, and it was this enemy which brought us together. The enemy is greed. I'm not talking here of a healthy determination to succeed; I'd be the first to admit that money is one of the more important motivations in my life. But our country has suffered in recent years from a different type of greed - unprincipled, evil self-interest. And sections of our government and judiciary seem determined to help it along its way.

We have all witnessed with shame the summer of scandals. As I write, the newspapers and television bring us more (is there anyone out there who hasn't had their telephone tapped?) Telecom, Greencore, the Beef Tribunal .. and now Gibgate. We hear scandalous calls from politicians for us to abandon all investigation into this rotten web of corruption, for it is damaging Ireland's reputation abroad and bringing shame on us all. The alternative to public inquiry is left to our cynical guesswork.

Ireland's corruption has wounded its people. For most, it reaches us indirectly, through the media. We read of the furtive evasions, we hear the downright lies, and we think of it as another world, a private club where the only qualifications for membership are wealth, greed and boundless immorality. How many laws are twisted and broken each day within a mile of Leinster House? I fear that calculation would be beyond my abilities.

It took this case to make me realise that this "other world" belongs to us, too. More than money has been stolen from us; we have been robbed of our pride.

I have called this book "Gibgate". I might just as easily have used our own country as the villain in the title.

Today is September 18, 1992. As I write these final words I can feel no certainty they will ever be read publicly. Those who would gain most from stopping its publication are well equipped to try and do so. But presuming that you're reading it now as an interested member of the public (and not as a judge about to slap me into prison) I can only tell you I hope it has done its job.

Despite everything which tells me I shouldn't, I've decided to keep working on the case of International Investments. This book is the beginning of the fight back. I pray there won't be any need for a follow-up.

Gibgate II? God forbid.

Billy Flynn

Rathcore, County Meath September 18, 1992